VEGETABLES: THE ARTIST AND THE GARDENER

Sue Goodchild

ARTHUR H. STOCKWELL LTD
Torrs Park, Ilfracombe, Devon, EX34 8BA
Established 1898
www.ahstockwell.co.uk

British Library Cataloguing-in-Publication Data.
A catalogue record for this book is available
from the British Library.

ISBN 978-0-7223-5154-3
Printed in Great Britain by
Arthur H. Stockwell Ltd
Torrs Park   Ilfracombe
Devon EX34 8BA

ACKNOWLEDGEMENTS

I am extremely grateful for the profound knowledge and assistance of dear friends Catherine Webstar and Robin Kempster in providing editorial advice and for making it fun and to my husband, Paul Goodman, without whom I would never have built the new greenhouse.

INTRODUCTION

A sketchbook in one hand and the other hand dislodging a weed, each slows down the other. All I ever wanted to do was to paint, and gardening is an extension of that passion. I have a sense of completeness, of simple happiness, between studio and garden. The garden is a place of quiet beauty giving delight, satisfaction and repose as well as exercise to mind and body. Just as the paintings display my love of nature and who I am, so does the garden, which would not exist otherwise.

My father studied horticulture at Southampton University and continued his love of gardening throughout life. As a child I spent a lot of time with grandparents absorbing their enthusiasm and knowledge. Grandfather grew chrysanthemums – huge, perfect blooms for sale in the flower shops. Each plant was rigidly tied to canes and regularly trimmed and any side shoots taken off, to achieve the supreme domed head to each plant. This idealism didn't appeal to me. It seemed that the plants were inflexible, unbending, held in their constraints. The results were fabulous, flawless with a beauty of their own. Somehow they appeared more beautiful when cut and grouped together. More natural-looking. Uncle Mick not a biological uncle, but my grandparents' lodger of decades and an important part of the family – preferred to grow tomatoes in the greenhouse. He taught me about their care and which were the sweetest. Grandmother loved roses. I have fond memories of roses around the window of my bedroom at their house. The beauty and scent of the climbing roses along with the serenade from blackbirds will always stay with me. Along with her love of roses, hydrangeas were planted along the wall. Their fabulous blue colour was due to the prodigious amount of tea leaves given to them each day. Everybody shared in tending the flower garden, so full of roses and sweet-smelling plants, a delight to sit in and draw on all the scents and beauty. I was so proud to bring my friends to this haven of delight.

With each successive house, I have created a garden, often dealing with wild, unkempt scrub. When my husband and I moved to France to create a painting school, we renovated the house and cleared the wild garden. We built paths and retaining walls, a herb garden, a swimming pool and beyond this a vegetable garden. Being south-facing and with the protection of the swimming-pool walls, the bananas flowered and produced fruit, but the season was not long enough for them to ripen. However, the vegetables were also protected and fared well.

While running the courses, we bought a ruin with tumbledown walls, no roof and a garden full of rubble, rocks, stones and brambles. As the ruin was not far from the main house, from time to time we were able to rebuild and tame the garden, and installing a potting shed and tool shed. We built a studio for me and a workshop/ garage for Paul, installed underfloor heating, demolished broken-down outhouses, moved tons of rock, created a wildlife pond and laid out the vegetable garden and flower borders. After turning a heap of stone into a home we moved in. I hated leaving the 'big' house and garden, but after twenty years of running the courses we decided to move to the smaller house.

Choosing the perfect location for the vegetable garden was important. As we live on a hill, it needed to be sheltered from the north wind. It is protected on two sides, east and south, by a copse of cherry, hawthorn, oak, chestnut, lime and holly and a lot of brambles. This gives food and shelter to wildlife such as hedgehogs, and gives us shelter from the east wind, though not from the prevailing south-west wind. Some years ago when visiting a château garden with my sister, Mag, I collected some black walnuts which germinated well and are now planted on the west side of the vegetable garden. These trees are important, but they do not stop the wind, which can be ferocious. Being on a hill, or really a plateau, it also means that the soil is free-draining. Few vegetables are drought-tolerant, so a water source needed to be close by. There is an old well on the boundary – its position on a hill is a puzzle, especially since it is not efficient, but then watercourses change with time. Perhaps in past years there was a useful water source. Now we have numerous barrels which collect water from guttering, as well as having a mains water supply to use when absolutely necessary. As the ground is very stony, with rocks big enough to edge the flower borders, raised beds seemed a good decision. The raised beds have improved the structure of the soil from years of adding compost, and are designed so that I can reach the centres of the beds from either side. To start with, I used wooden planks, but these dried and disintegrated in the heat of the summer assisted by insects and wet in the winter. We now have home-made edgings, which look decorative and do the job well. Home-made compost and a friend's horse have built up the fertility, and the raised beds warm faster in spring.

As vegetables come from all parts of the world, they need different growing conditions. Man with his ingenuity has been breeding and selecting varieties of these plants so that they can grow side by side and flourish even though they have different needs. The gardener has to learn what is needed and when. Carrots and parsnips must have good straight roots, but if grown in newly manured ground will fork and become misshapen, while given these conditions brassicas, including sprouts, cabbages, broccoli, kale and radishes, will thrive. Potatoes need to be good tubers, peas have to be grown from good seeds, and runner beans and courgettes need plenty of compost at their roots to produce a good crop.

Companion planting is worth considering as some plants enjoy the same conditions. Cabbages and Brussel sprouts, or roots such as beetroot and lettuce, are good companions, drawing nutrients from different depths in the soil. Beans and cucumbers, or leeks and celery, or runner beans and bush tomatoes, all enjoy rich, moist soil and take advantage of light at different levels. Squashes, courgettes and pumpkins provide moisture-retentive ground cover for sweetcorn while suppressing weeds. Lettuces draw lightly from the soil and grow well under runner beans, so making use of an awkward area. Interplanting cool-loving lettuce among sweetcorn, aubergines and peppers, maximises use of space. Monoculture encourages bugs but companion planting can also confuse unwanted bugs, with different scents. Aphids prefer lush green foliage, so placing crops like beans interplanted with purple, red or blue crops, such as red cabbage, red kale, purple sprouting broccoli or ruby chard, can confuse. Growing tomatoes, beans and cucumbers among brassicas confuses beetles. Aromatic herbs such as garlic and chives, act as a barrier and I ring vulnerable plants with calendula, tagetes, nasturtiums, basil, caraway and other spicy herbs. Growing a variety of plants attracts predators. Gardeners learn that nectar-rich flowers, such as sweet peas, poppies, forget-me-nots, feverfew, violas, fennel or marigolds, encourage natural predators like hoverflies, which lay their eggs on the plants and their larvae eat the aphids and other pests. I let these flowering plants self-seed so that they appear in the vegetable garden and the flower garden.

We are very fortunate in that we live in a mild climate, but even so the polytunnel and greenhouse are invaluable. I grow salads all year. In spring, crops of lettuces, early peas and carrots are followed by melons, basil and peppers, and in winter they provide shelter for tender plants and numerous cuttings. A cloche within the tunnel in very cold weather gives extra protection. It is important to choose the right crops for the right conditions as in summer the heat can be overpowering and in winter humidity is a problem. Ventilation is crucial. Once light levels improve in spring, the tunnel is the ideal place for seedlings which can grow quickly in the protected area. The soil in the tunnel needs to be replaced every spring. I take out the top layer of old soil and add a top dressing of fresh compost, and water well before any planting takes place. This gives the soil time to settle and encourages earthworms.

As seedlings become ready to plant outdoors, a few can be planted in the tunnel, where they will be ready to harvest several weeks earlier than outside. I grow various flowers in the tunnel to attract pollinating insects such as hoverflies and hawkmoths, which love nicotiana.

Rotation is important. Plants belong to families, and a

disease of one plant can affect other plants in the same family. Clubroot, a well-known disease of cabbages, can be passed on through the soil if another member of the cabbage family, such as broccoli, is grown in the same place in the following season, but will have no effect on potatoes. Potato blight can affect tomatoes – a close relative of the potato – but has no effect on beans. The rotation system prevents many pests and diseases with a three-year rotation plan, but five is better. One group of vegetables is grown in each plot and in subsequent years moved to another plot. Some plants can improve the soil – for instance, peas and beans have nodules on their roots containing bacteria that can stabilise nitrogen extracted from the air. If the roots are left in the ground after harvest, the following crop can benefit. Different crops take different elements from the soil, so rotating them allows the soil to recover its nutrient status. These nutrients keep crops healthier, so that they are better able to shrug off pests.

Planning the garden rotation is much the same as planning a painting. The thought prior to sowing and planting is the same as composing a sketch. The design is all-important. I sketch out a plan of the garden with each raised bed to be planted, ticking off permanently planted beds, such as asparagus. It is also important to plan sowing times so that there are not too many similar vegetables maturing at the same time. It is best to sow in smaller quantities at intervals through the season so that cropping follows one after another. Winter and spring crops need time to grow through the year as they mature slowly. Lettuce and beetroot when harvested make room for growing winter crops. This way there is not so much of a glut with one crop following on from another.

Many plants, both ornamental and edible, can be sown directly into seedbeds or first raised in pots then transplanted. Some, however, resent this disturbance and need to be sown direct to thrive. Vegetables such as carrots and parsnips hate root disturbance. Transplanting can damage the delicate taproots or fine hairs and put the plants into shock. Success with direct sowing requires good soil preparation and only sowing when the ground is warm enough.

We are surrounded by fields which are not as attractive to 'pests' as the delicious plants in the garden, but slugs and snails attract blackbirds, thrushes and hedgehogs, and other small birds feed on aphids. So long as the plants are healthy, they can recover from attacks; and, of course, we love to see the different creatures thriving.

The paintings have to be done fairly quickly unless painted in situ because once picked, leaves deteriorate and roots dry out. I start with a pencil drawing, working out the composition and planning colours and tones, giving a shape with which to work. Most sketches are in watercolour or graphite.

The vegetable garden is a place of beauty – a lovely place to wander and find luscious fruits plucked straight from the plant. There is something sensual about growing things, enjoying the sight, the smells and the tastes of all around. The garden is a work in progress as it evolves and changes, and painting is the same, project after project. Learning comes with each new experience, and with knowledge comes the realisation that there is always more to learn, more to experience.

This book is derived from personal experience and with love of all that I do – painting and gardening. My aim is to capture these magical moments on paper or canvas in a way that is not possible by photography.

Painting 1 and the Gardener

A view from my studio. The vegetable garden is more than just a collection of edible plants. I wanted it to be beautiful and planned for all-year interest as well as intrigue. This is part of the interest to paint the garden. Due to the complicated nature of the subject, a sketch sorted out the composition, which was followed by a layout in pencil on watercolour paper.

As is obvious from the painting, I love blue – bright, cheerful and making the subject appealing to the artistic eye. The blue pots are adorned with blue agapanthus flowers later in the season and the fabulous morning glory climbs the archway. These are complemented by the stunning yellow of the courgette flowers with marigold and tagetes a bright addition among the plants as well as being a deterrent to destructive insects. Other flowers, such as amaranthus, attract bees, hoverflies and butterflies, for example insects needed for pollinating fruit and vegetables. Amaranthus has thousands of seeds which fall and germinate in all the borders, giving a splash of colour. Climbing beans and sweet peas climb the tripods, and are also good for attracting pollinators.

The archways are constantly buffeted by the south-west winds. Whenever I look at the archways, I am reminded of a dear friend who kindly pointed out that perspective needs attention, but with the wonky nature of the structure and the painting being in watercolour it is difficult to alter. Had the medium been oil or pastel, the change could have been made.

In the background of the painting are joster berries, kindly donated by Sarah, a dear friend, with cabbage, broccoli, chard, peas, parsnips, strawberries and lettuces, just indicated due to distance. To the left of the painting,

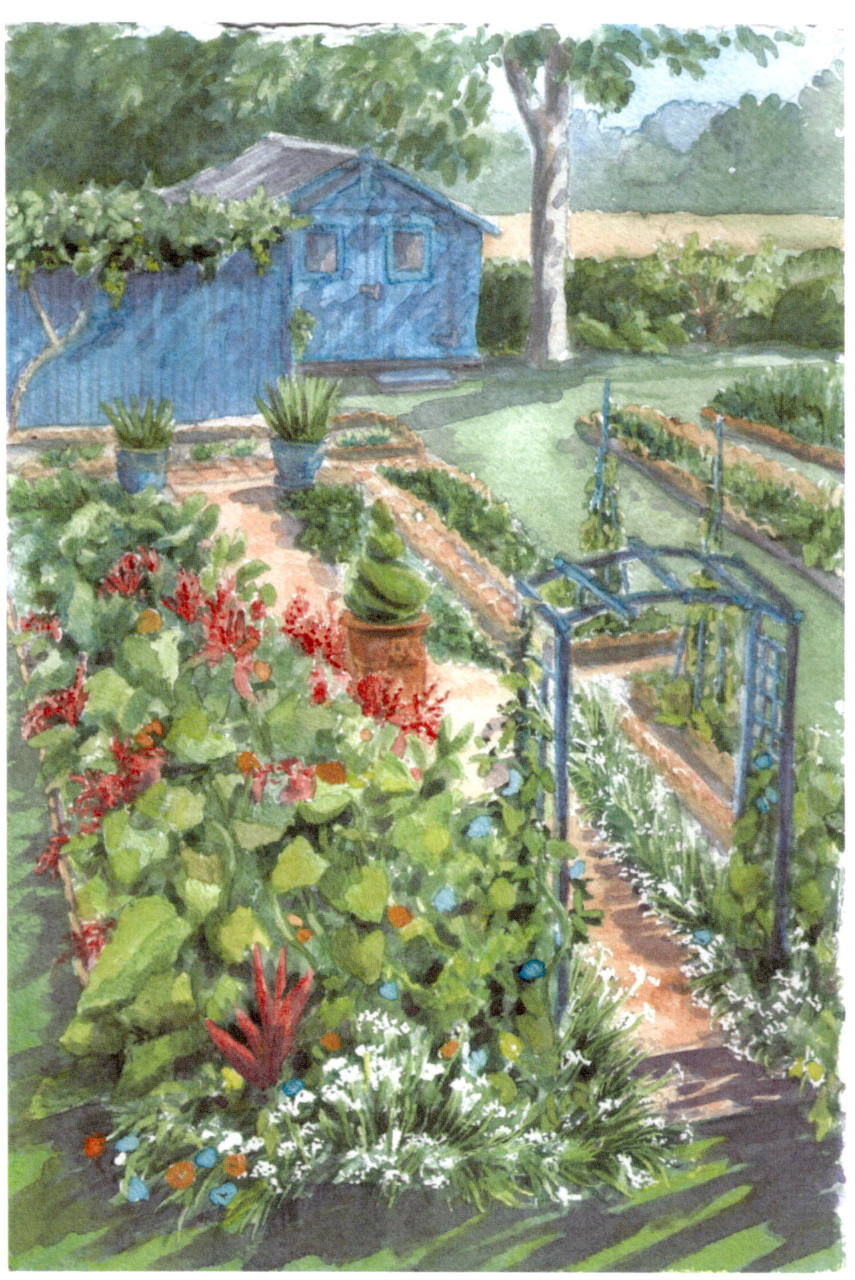

out of the picture, are espalier apple, peach, apricot, raspberries and the asparagus bed.

The structure of the vegetable garden was planned with grass walkways, some gravel and some with terracotta tiles gleaned from the old house. Paul made the edgings. They hold the compost better than wood surrounds, which dry out and crack in the hot, dry summers and rot in the wet winters. The blue shed holds the tools and the blue fence supports the very productive grapevine. The old lime tree next to the shed has suffered with the high winds, continually shedding branches and twigs, and is not helped by the increasing mistletoe. It is, after all, older than the copse beyond. Surrounding the copse and garden is a field grazed by cows which glows with colour from wild flowers; but with the south-west wind, seeds of weeds such as the lesser celandine, a beautiful plant but invasive, blow into the garden.

When I first planted the garden, I edged the paths with chives, loving the purple flowers as well as their culinary use, but an infestation of blackfly weakened the plants and garlic chives took over. Some chives survive and as these flower at different times from the garlic chives I can enjoy them both.

Painting 2 and the Gardener

This painting sometime later shows the same view but with different plants and the slate, dug up from the ground, now laid along the paths. The chives still flourish, as does the rose painted with Permanent Rose. I used very few colours: Yellow Ochre for the pots and diluted for the border edges, Ultramarine blue for the archway with Cerulean Blue in sunlit places, and Lemon Yellow mixed into the blue to create the green. Ultramarine Violet adjusted with yellow was used for the slate in the paths and shadows. This mixed colour of violet and yellow was added to the green for the darks where the leaves cast shadows. The sunflowers, defying the wind, were painted with Lemon Yellow with a little ochre for the one forming seeds. There is an addition of artichoke with most other crops grown in different beds. Crop rotation is most important for successful soil management, and hence the borders change every year. When the blue fence and the vine blew down, I saw it as an opportunity to rethink, and I now have a large greenhouse in its place and cuttings of the vine grow in a more sheltered part of the garden.

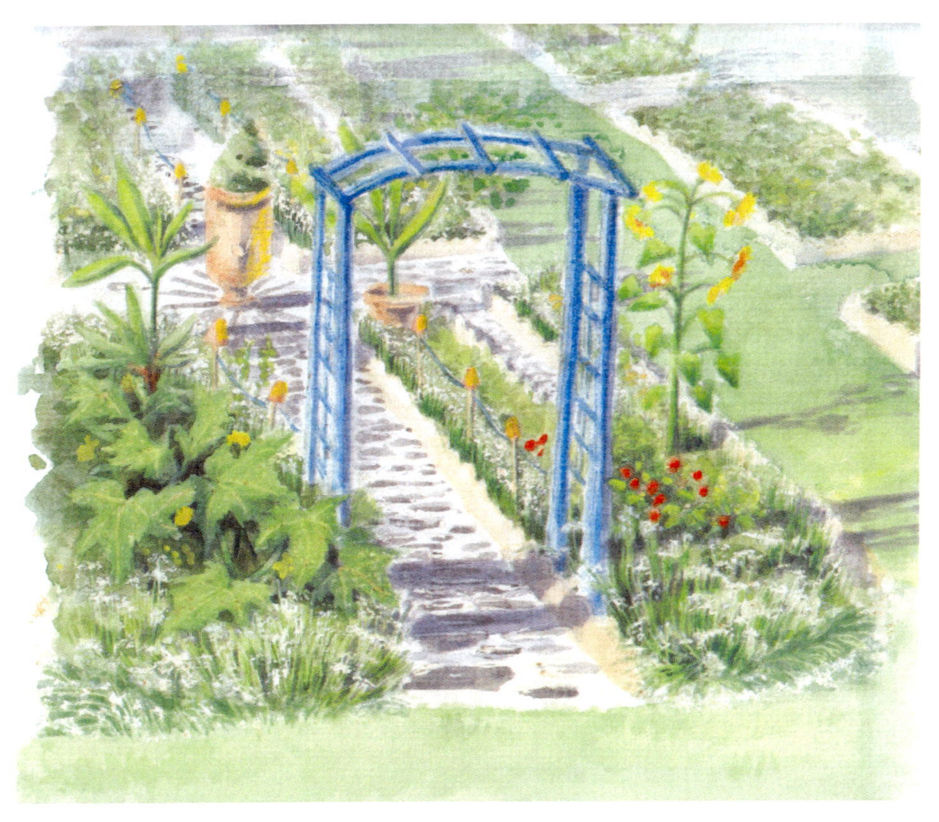

THE OIL PAINTING

Purple and blue are my favourite colours, so it is not surprising that I was inspired to paint cabbages and marigolds, each enhancing the colour of the other. Colour is very powerful in stimulating emotion, lifting the spirits and creativity.

To start with, a thumbnail sketch determines the composition and the value studies. These are quick drawings concentrating on tonal values and shapes, not detailed drawings, especially since outdoor light is not controllable. Shadows move and the light can be unpredictable. The goal of the composition is to direct attention to the main objective, and in this composition I decided on a horizontal format, grouped the cabbages closer together and multiplied the amount of marigold surrounding them. The leaves are the dominate shapes and determine the overall composition.

Curved forms, such as cabbage leaves, lit from one side have a darker, shadowed side giving them a sense of depth. Dark colours are laid in first as they lose their strength to underlying lighter colours. As the painting progresses, the amount of oil is increased – the thicker and more oily the mix the slower the drying time. It is important to lay thick over thin. When a layer of paint is applied to the canvas the oil slowly oxidises on contact with the air and forms a skin. This process occurs with each successive layer of paint, giving a special richness to the colours; and as the paint dries slowly, it can be manipulated using scumbles, short dabs and curving strokes, creating a brilliant impasto effect. This adds interest and impact balanced by simple, quiet passages rather than less predictable, quick, freer gestural marks. These thick, succulent marks are the last to be added, and only at the front of the painting.

I used a mix of blues and purples, interspersed with greens. The fence at the back of the vegetable plot was a cool blue, helping to give recession but with warmer, more purple shadows from the vine. This same blue was mixed with white for the high-lighted edges of the cabbage leaves. The marigolds were cool and warm yellows with dots of red in the foreground and just touched with colour on the cabbage leaves. When changing to a new colour the contents of the brush are squeezed out on to newspaper to remove the original colour. When continuing the painting the next day, the brushes should be suspended in white spirit without washing them and the next time squeezed on to a rag. Brushes can be washed with soap when the painting is finished.

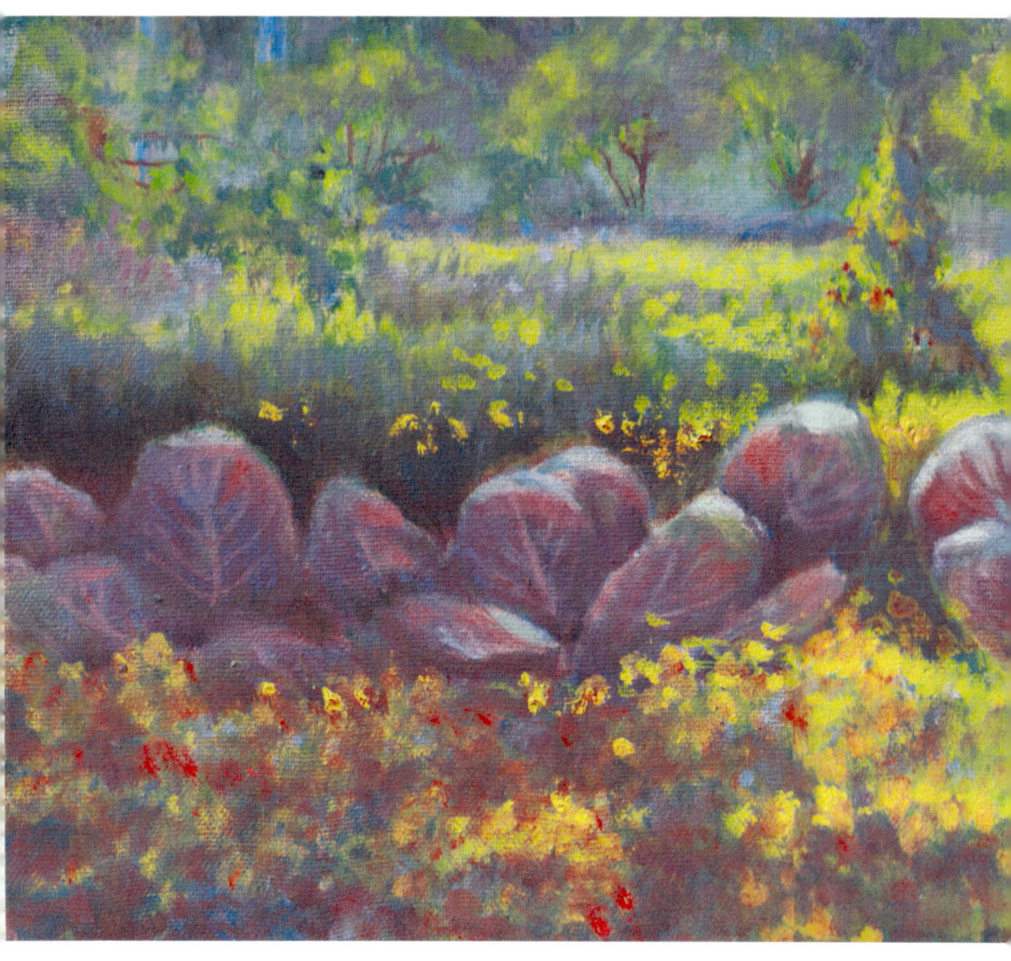

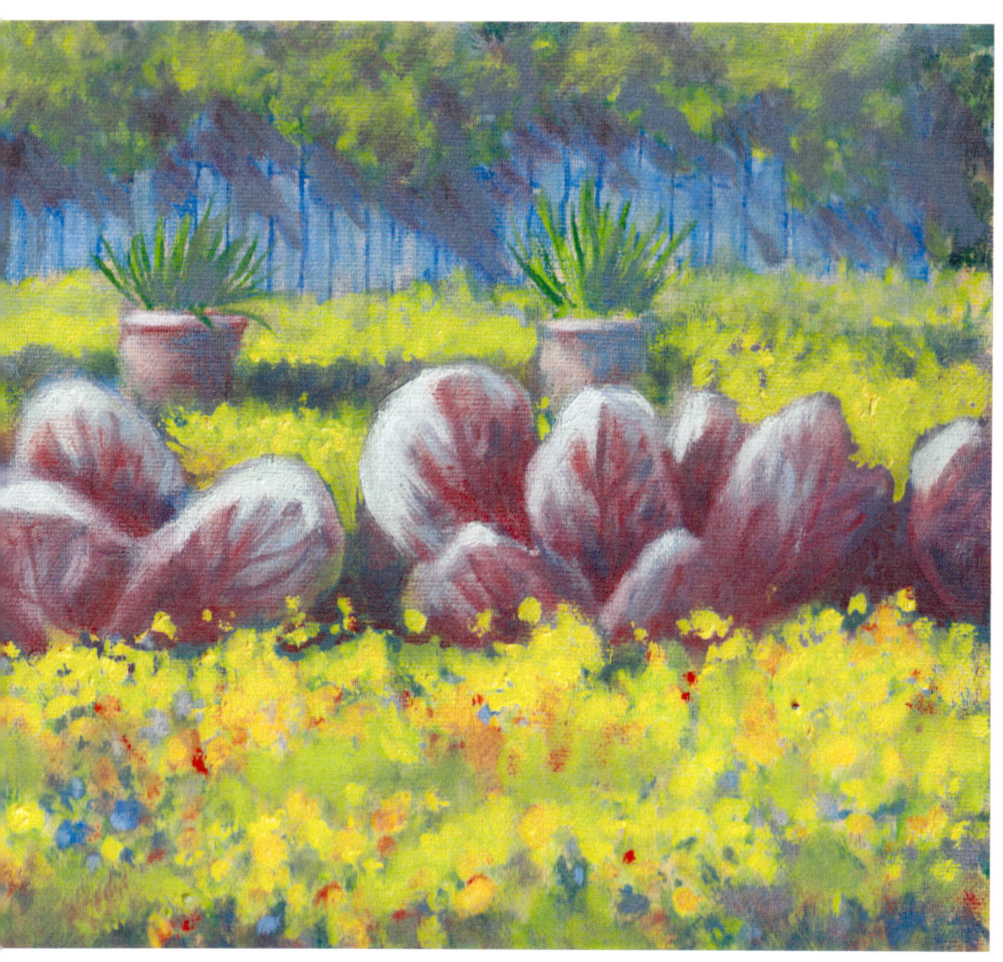

ASPARAGUS

The Paintings

I had to think carefully about the subject. Should I paint the shoots or the ferns, and how should I do it? I decided that the shoots looked beautiful in the early morning light and also a close-up version shows more clearly the structure of the shoots.

Painting 1

The cool, yellow morning light fell on to the left side, with the shadow on the right. I chose a complementary-coloured

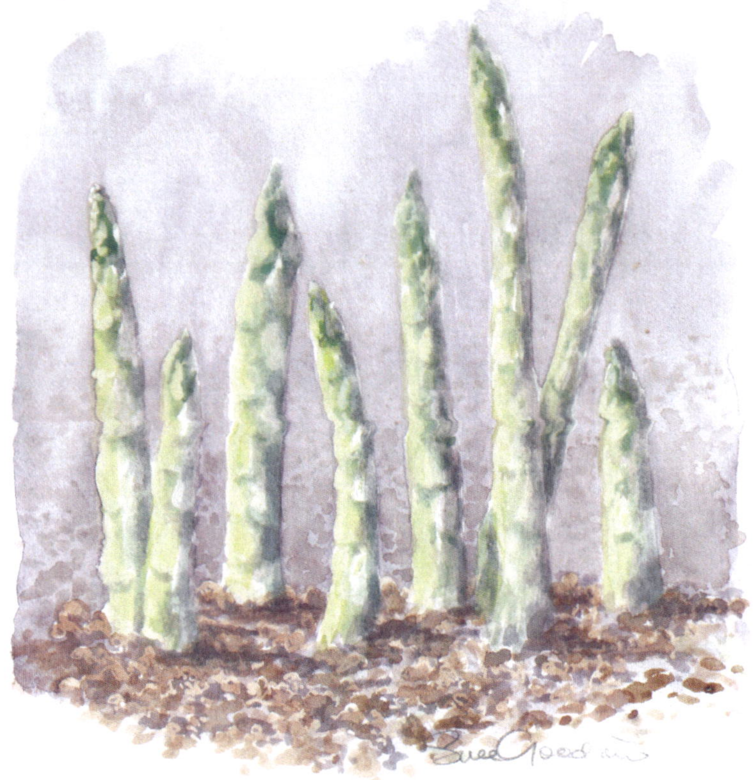

background to show up the yellow light. A little violet was added to Sap Green for the darkest areas of the shoots. The compost around the shoots was rough, so I used dabs of Burnt Sienna, Ultramarine Violet mixed into the Burnt Sienna, and Burnt Umber.

Painting 2

This close-up view, later in the day, gave me the opportunity to explore the tips and use pink and green together. The tips were mostly the white of the paper, shaded with pink and darkened with Quinacridone Rose and Sap Green. The main stalks were the same green run into the pink at the base and then the same dark on the right side. The straw at the base was masked first and then painted with Burnt Sienna and Burnt Umber. The background was a wash of green run into the Burnt Sienna so that they merged.

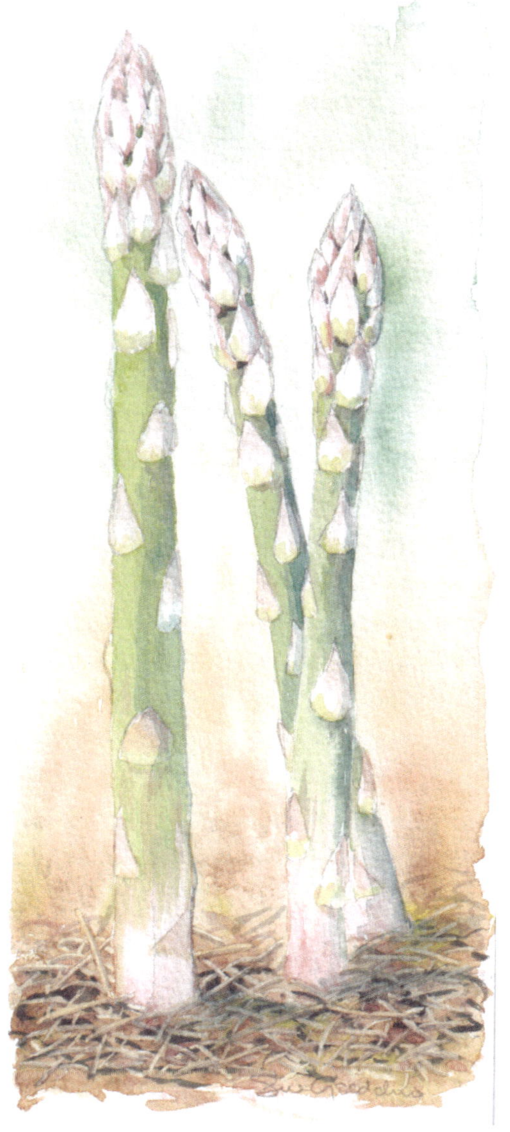

The Gardener

Asparagus has been prized in the Mediterranean region, found depicted on an Egyptian frieze dating to 3,000 BC Greeks and Romans cultivated it and ate it fresh in season and dried in the winter.

The most common varieties are green. White asparagus has been blanched by covering the young shoots with soil as they grow. It is called 'white gold', 'edible ivory' and the 'royal vegetable'. White asparagus is prized as a luxury vegetable, sweeter and more delicate than green varieties because of its higher sugar content. The purple variety is smaller and fruitier. The best shoots are the young tips as when these begin to branch and mature they become woody and bitter. Older plants have thicker stems. Cutting the stems is best done with a long, sharp knife, with the fingers following down the stem to cut below soil level. This must be done carefully as it is easy to damage younger, adjacent shoots not yet visible. They must be eaten fresh and should be harvested regularly before they become stringy. I like to eat them raw, snapping them off while working in the garden. An asparagus crown produces many small shoots at different stages of maturity. Cutting should cease by the end of June. A common reason for deterioration is cutting over too long a period with disregard to feathery fern production, which feeds the crowns.

The underground stems or rhizomes, shoots or spears, and roots, are used in medicine. Asparagus is used to treat bladder infections as it increases urine output. It can also reduce blood pressure and is used in the treatment of joint pain or rheumatism, hormone inbalance, dryness in lungs and throat, constipation, nerve pain and cancer. It can also be applied directly to the skin for cleansing the face, drying sores and treating acne. It is high in folic acid, and a good source of potassium, fibre, thiamin, vitamins A, B6, C and E, calcium, magnesium, zinc, iron, copper, manganese and selenium. It was believed that if a pregnant women ate asparagus she was more likely to give birth to a boy.

Asparagus may be propagated by sowing seed, with a three-year delay between sowing and cropping. Seed can be sown indoors in spring and seedlings transplanted into the permanent bed in the following year. One-year-old crowns, planted in April, have time to establish a good root system far more quickly than two- or three-year-old plants. No harvesting should be done in the first years so that the plant can build up crown size. Once established, asparagus, if well managed, will provide crops for twenty years or longer.

Male plants produce more and better spears as they do not put energy into seed production. Female plants have bell-shaped, greenish-white flowers, followed by small, red berries which are poisonous to humans. Asparagus has feathery foliage which, when it has died back in the autumn, can be cut down to ground level and mulched, building up the soil with mounds of organic compost. Asparagus roots tend to develop laterally, so it is best to maintain the food supply in the top of the soil. It grows best in an open, sunny position, though it will tolerate semi-shade. It is not particular about soil type, but favours a sandy loam and constant moisture but well-drained.

Tomatoes are planted with asparagus. They are good companion plants as tomatoes repel the asparagus beetle, which can severely damage the spears.

PURPLE SPROUTING BROCCOLI

The Paintings

The greatest challenge is not only discovering what is to be said in the painting, but how to communicate a shared visual experience. Degas said, "Art is not what you see but what you make others see." It is not the amount of hard work and perspiration for a painting to succeed, but deep passion and feeling of strong desire to achieve the goal. An artist is more likely to be successful when painting with passion.

Composition is extremely important as it is the framework of the painting. To start I make several simple drawings, without detail, to decide the composition, remembering that the negative shapes are just as important as the positive shapes. Line, shape, space, colour, tonal value, contrast and elements of design, how to place the focal point, which colours to use and with what intensity – all of these have to be considered before starting to paint.

Drawing the preparatory sketch is easier if the subject is a reality and not imagined. It gives a deeper insight into how to interpret the subject and express emotions. In my experience, this almost always results in more vitality than an abstract idea.

When painting the leaves, a single stroke of the brush has more freshness and immediacy than brushstrokes that are overworked or manipulated and can be a powerful way of bringing life to a painting. A round brush which has a tip as well as a body is useful as it holds plenty of pigment and a single stroke can suffice. It can also go from thick to thin and pale to dark depending on the pressure applied.

The leaves in this painting were made with successive washes built up to the darks in the shadows and the

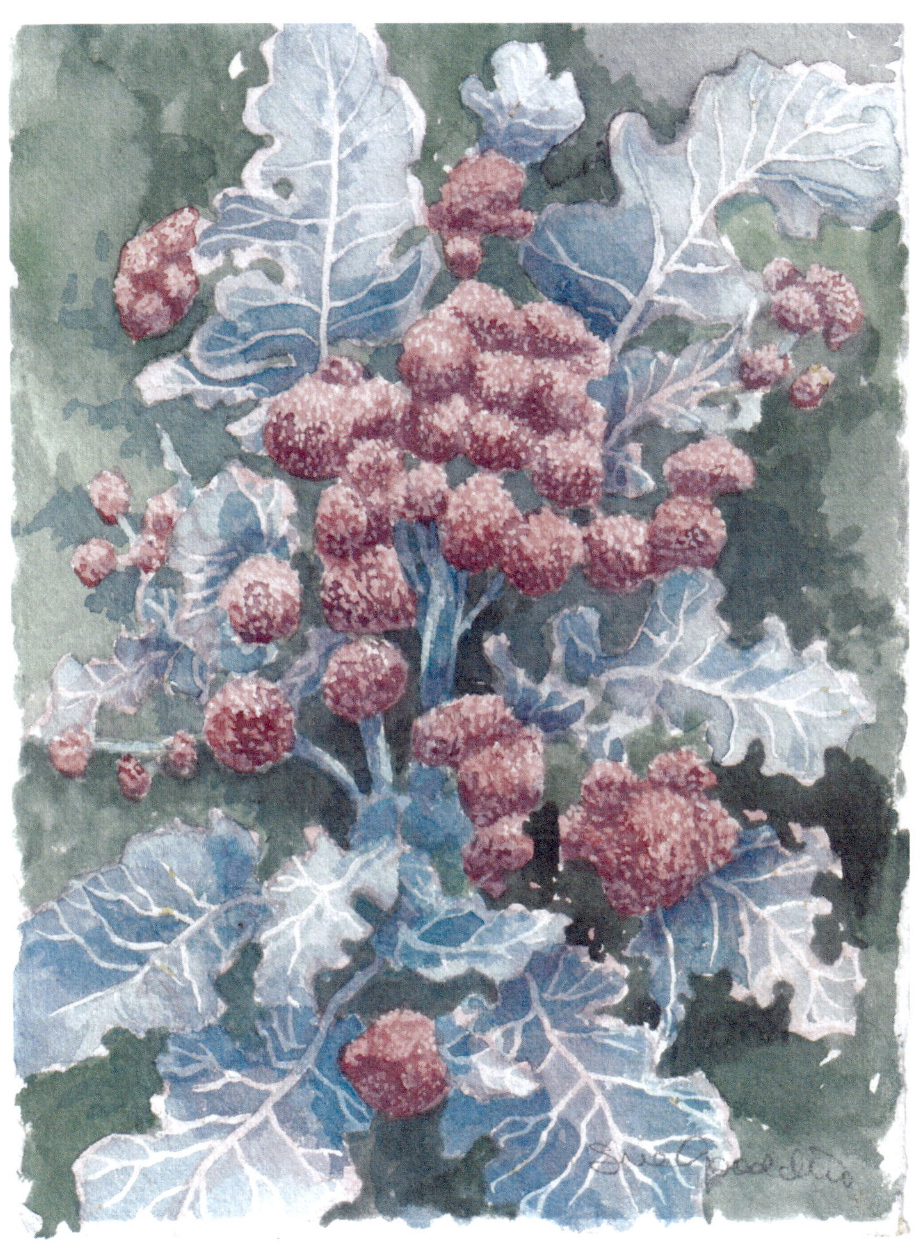

broccoli heads were masked with dabs of fluid and then spattered with purple.

The Gardener
Different parts of brassicas – leaves, stems, buds and flowers – have been developed for eating, providing textures, shapes, colours and tastes. Purple sprouting broccoli is grown for its succession of slender flower shoots, which are snapped off before the buds open and best harvested regularly, stimulating production of more florets. Good compost is important as organic materials support many organisms that result in strong, healthy plants which can fight diseases, and attract the beneficial insects and repel those not wanted.

BROCCOLI

The Gardener
The term *broccoli* is a plural form of the Italian meaning 'cabbage top'. It is related to sprouting broccoli. It is easier to grow than cauliflower and is much hardier and less demanding in its soil requirements, doing well in good, fertile soil though not needing freshly manured soil. Broccoli makes a good follow-on crop to peas and beans as they are planted out in mid to late summer. Raised beds provide better conditions for germination and growth. Broccoli is best sown in spring and when planted out should be given plenty of space as it grows to be a big plant. In our garden broccoli has to be planted deeply and firmly because of the south-west wind, which can bend or even uproot the plants. The florets should be picked continually as this stimulates the plant to produce

more heads. The tight flower heads should be picked with no leaves so that they sprout again for further pickings. Picking them when young stops them blooming, but eventually yellow flowers appear in spring.

CALABRESE

Calabrese is a green form of broccoli, also known as Italian sprouting broccoli. Some varieties have a large central conical head which after harvesting produces a number of side shoots. The seeds should be sown in spring, with plants maturing in autumn and early winter. I grow 'Romanesco' which has yellow-green florets, but it is a large plant and takes up a lot of space with a small harvest.

CAULIFLOWER

The Painting
I don't usually use white paint, but in this depiction of a cauliflower it seemed practical to dab gouache over the slightly purple-brown watercolour. Watercolour is a transparent medium, so the white needed to be opaque, as with gouache. It is easy to use, being essentially between watercolour and acrylic. Unlike acrylic, gouache can be altered and manipulated like watercolour and remains viable at a later date. Unlike watercolour, because of its opaque nature it can be painted light on top of dark; but as it remains water-soluble, care must be taken not to disturb the underlying paint. In this case I wanted the paint to be thick, so used less water. White is the most important colour in watercolour. It makes all the other colours glow.

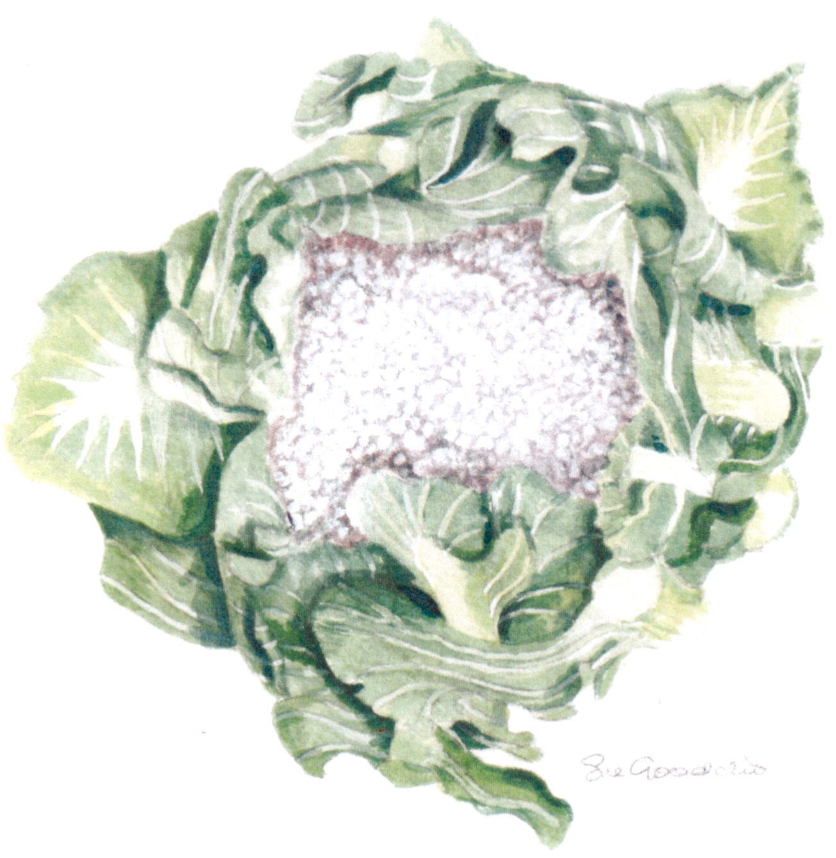

There is a challenge in each painting to eliminate just enough of the white paper to achieve the perfect balance. In this case I am adding white not reserving white paper. For the stems and veins in the leaves I used masking fluid to reserve the white paper, added the green and then toned with a very dilute yellow green.

These procedures needed planning. Oscar Wilde wrote, 'I was working on the proof of one of my poems all the morning, and took out a comma. In the afternoon I put it back in.' It is the same with painting, but to retain freshness planning is necessary in watercolour as it is not easy to change things.

The Gardener

Cauliflowers are gross feeders, liking rich, deep loam, and will not thrive on heavy, badly drained or very light soils which dry out in summer, or poor, hungry ground. In autumn compost or manure should be dug into a sunny site sheltered from cold winds. Those for harvesting in midsummer should be sown in mid autumn and overwintered under glass. Those for cutting in mid autumn are sown in mid to late spring, and those for late autumn are sown in early summer. A glut can be avoided by making two sowings with two weeks between, as cauliflower seed remains viable for several years, and sowing can be staggered. The heads can be successfully frozen. In our dry garden, watering in a drought is essential; otherwise the plants will go to seed.

When the plants are growing strongly, I give them a dose of liquid manure with the appearance of weak tea at weekly or two-weekly intervals. The florets quickly form, but sunlight can turn the curds yellow. To prevent this, I snap the stems of a few of the outer leaves and fold them over the developing curd to shut out the light. The same procedure can be used to protect them from frost. Modern varieties have been bred to 'self-protect' as the inner leaves fold automatically over the curd.

If the soil is dry, water well prior to lifting. This will help to keep the cauliflower in good condition for about a week in a cool, dark place. The plant supplies selenium and vitamin C.

BRUSSEL SPROUTS

The Painting

The shadows on each sprout and on the stem and leaves give a feeling of form, both for the individual sprout and as a group as part of the whole plant. The light was coming from the side, but also leaves and sprouts cast shadows on to their neighbours. Deeper tonal marks show form. One shape explains another, all connected together as a continual shape. Contrast attracts the eye. Once understood, it can be used to suggest different moods. Lots of contrast suggests a sunny, bright day while tones close in value create a moody, perhaps misty or overcast effect. If a painting doesn't have any depth, it is often because the tones are wrong.

Constructive criticism of one's own work must be honest, and not judgemental, but a productive assessment of the work will help the artist to see what is needed to improve, and recognise when to congratulate. Putting the painting aside for a while helps me to see it with fresh eyes and become aware if any changes are necessary. It could be now that I need to exaggerate the dark tone to give a more lively effect and greater depth.

The Gardener

Brussel sprouts need plenty of nourishment and will not do well in poor soils, so preparation by incorporating farmyard manure or compost is important. Many gardeners consider that sprouts taste much better after frost, which means sowing in spring, planting out in early summer or midsummer. The seed should be sown in February or sown direct under cloches from March. The seed should be sown very thinly into plugs or trays and labelled. I write the name of the plant in pencil so that the labels can be washed and

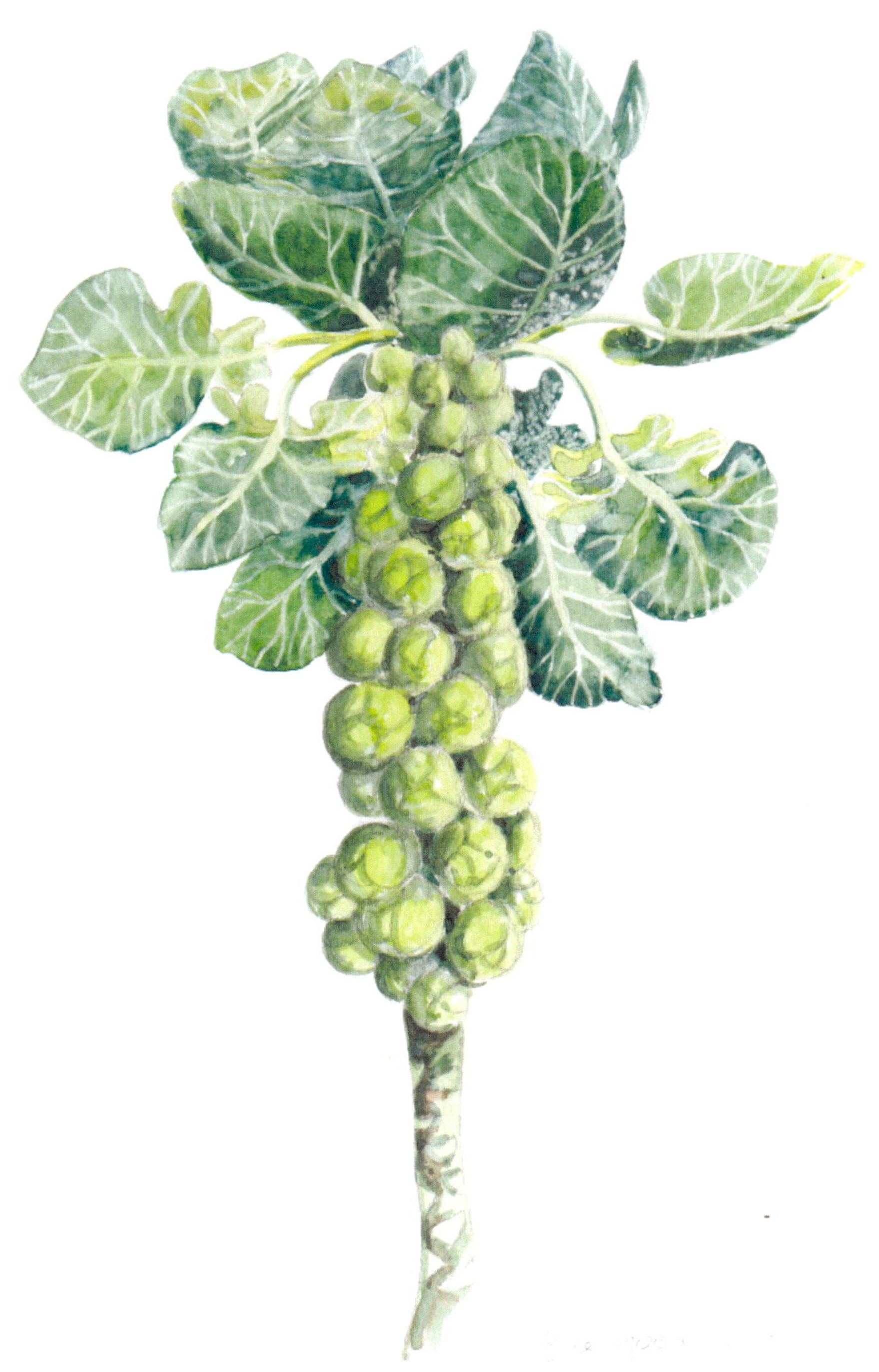

used again. Seed compost should have little nutrition, and when seedlings are large enough they should be potted into compost with more goodness to promote healthy roots. When conditions are right for the plant, they can be accustomed to cooler temperatures in the cold frame before planting out in late spring to early summer in a sunny sheltered area. It is important to plant firmly with the lower leaves just clear of the soil. Sprouts need room in which to mature. In our windy site, I stake the plants as well as drawing a little soil up to the plants to give them good anchorage.

Any leaves that go yellow should be snapped off and composted, as leaving them could cause mould or rot. To harvest the sprouts, snap the buttons off with a downward pressure of the thumb, picking from the base upwards. 'Blown' sprouts are those which remain open and do not form a 'button'. Loose soil is often the cause. It is important that no sprouts are allowed to flower and seed, as this is when most nourishment is taken from the soil. The top heads make a cabbage-like vegetable. These can be harvested in spring, when their winter protection is no longer needed.

Brussel sprouts are high in folic acid, vitamis B2, A and K and minerals. They also have cancer-fighting chemicals – particularly colon cancer. An average serving contains four times more vitamin C than an orange.

ROCKET

The Painting
The initial leaves of the plant were started with watercolour using Lemon Yellow with a little Ultramarine Blue. The foreground was a wash of Burnt Sienna and Yellow Ochre merged into Ultramarine Blue in the background. With

pastel pencils, I picked up the yellow green of the main leaves and used various greens, cool and warm, in between and behind and the darkest, bluest green at the back. This same dark green was dragged lightly over the foreground and background to unify the whole.

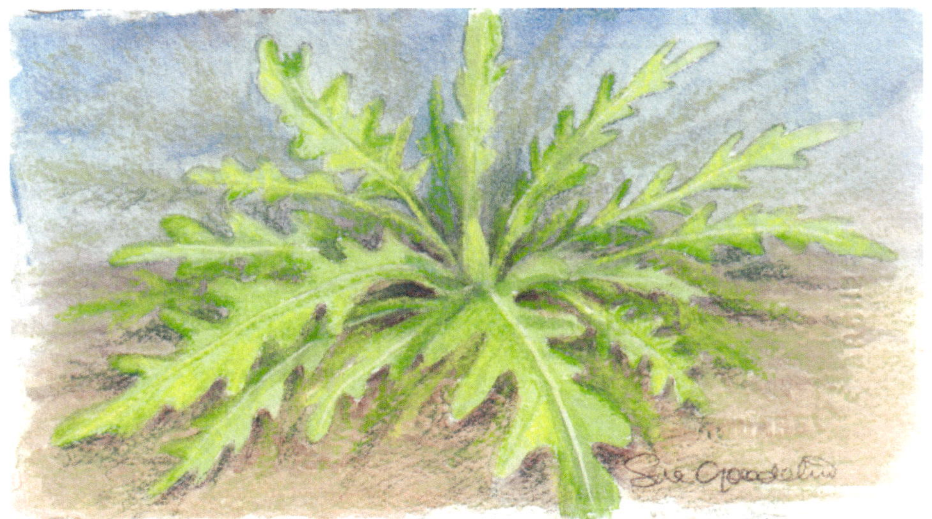

When assessing the painting, more lemon was added in places on the leaves. Sometimes the patterns created by dappled light can explain a subject without painting the plant itself.

The Gardener

As rocket dislikes root disturbance, the seed should be sown thinly, directly into good, fertile soil or a pot and kept moist and shaded in summer heat to avoid bolting. Rocket is best sown every few weeks for a harvest throughout summer and autumn as a 'cut and come again' crop. Spring and autumn sowings tend to be more successful. I provide shade in summer to prevent bolting. Late summer sowings survive winter if under cover, producing new tangy leaves and edible flowers in spring. Timing of seed sowing is important because if it is too early seeds may not germinate, and left too late the resulting plants may not have enough time to mature.

When eaten raw, rocket contains high levels of vitamins C, A, B and K and folic acid, calcium and potassium. The flowers are also nutritious and can be added to salads. Rocket has three times the amount of nitrates than beetroot. Regular harvesting encourages regrowth and more cuttings.

Wild rocket, *Diplotaxis tenuifolia*, is perennial and has a stronger taste and serrated leaves. Salad rocket, *eruca vesicaria*, is quick-growing but short-lived.

LETTUCE

The Painting

Monochrome paintings have a simple beauty with different textures and shapes created with a round brush which has a good tip. A single stroke has more freshness and immediacy, indicating movement or a sense of direction, than one that is overworked or manipulated.

The flow through a painting can be soft, such as a curve or changes of direction, as in the roundness of the lettuce leaves leading one into another. The rhythmic lines and shapes take the eye around the painting.

Each leaf was painted on damp paper, which gives a soft appearance and avoids hard lines. Watercolour paint dries lighter than it initially appears when wet. It is easy to think that it is best to start the painting very light and build up the colour later; but to avoid the painting being pale and washed out, the colour should be more intense with more pigment in the mixture.

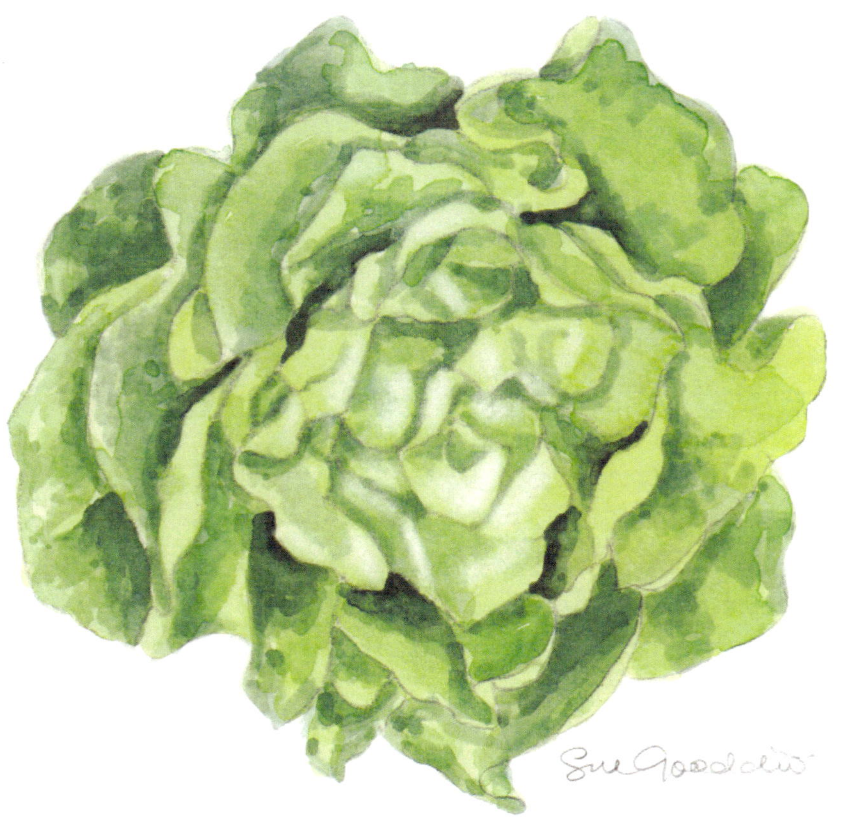

The Gardener

I don't remember the last time I bought lettuce. When harvesting from the garden I cut lettuce leaves rather than pull the whole plant, as they will regrow. There are colours of light green, blue green, red, deep purple and dark green and mottled colours. The variety Buttercrunch has dark-green leaves, is sweet, crisp and pleasant-tasting. It is widely grown in Europe, but how much better it is to have it fresh from the garden! Loose-leaf varieties have tender, flavourful and delicate leaves. There are varieties Red Oak Leaf and Green Oak Leaf. Lamb Lettuce has long spoon-shaped dark leaves and a tangy flavour; and

Crisphead varieties, also called 'iceberg' lettuce, have tight, dense heads similar to cabbage, but the lowest nutritional value. Romaine lettuce varieties, also called 'cos', have long heads of sturdy leaves, and are the most nutritious.

The darker the lettuce, the more nutrient-dense it is as it contains more antioxidants, which contribute to its anti-inflammatory properties. Lettuce provides calcium, potassium, vitamin C, K and A, folate, and helps fight diseases like cancer. Vitamin A in lettuce revitalises the skin, and this increases cell turnover as well as the development of new bone cells. The potassium in lettuce improves circulation, supplying oxygen and other nutrients to the skin, and vitamin C can protect the skin from UV radiation, delaying the signs of ageing and with vitamin A, helps oxidisze cholesterol and strengthen the arteries, both improving blood flow and preventing heart attacks. The fibre in lettuce is also good to detox the system, which leads to glowing skin. Vitamin K boosts hair strength and can prevent hair loss.

Lettuce is easily cultivated, requiring low temperatures to prevent it from flowering quickly, though there are summer varieties. It is hard to judge the amount of seed in a row, but the plants can be thinned and these thinnings transplanted or eaten. To avoid slug damage it is a good idea to sow a few seeds every few weeks into modules and plant seedlings into the garden. This also avoids a glut. When the plants start to 'bolt', they begin to taste bitter.

Lettuce was originally cultivated in Ancient Egypt for the extraction of oil from its seeds. There is evidence of the plant in 2680 BC and it is recorded in medieval writings from 1098 to 1179, mentioned as a medicinal herb. It was taken to America by Christopher Columbus in the late fifteenth century.

PEAS

The Painting

It took four days to design, paint and assess this picture, by which time the peas had been eaten. My first idea was for the peas to curve across the page with another plant below; but because of the amount of detail in the pea plant, I changed the initial composition and chose vegetable beds and a path leading the eye into the painting. The angle of the path was important to give balance to the leaning pea plant.

I drew the pea plant and set the angles of the path and then used an Ultramarine Blue and Phthalo Blue wash into the pre-wet sky area. I mixed green from Ultramarine Blue and Lemon Yellow for the various vegetable borders, making sure that the background bed was faint and misty-looking so as not to compete with the peas. The path was washed with weak Ultramarine Violet, and everything was left to dry before swirling in pea stems, tendrils and leaves. The pea pods were painted with a lemony green on one side and, while still wet, a mid green down the centre with a deeper, darker green on the shadow side. Many more leaves and stems were added and plants suggested in the other borders.

When all was dry, many more darks were added to leaves along the shadow side of the stems and tendrils, and to the pods, making sure that the peas were darker and more prominent than the rest of the painting. More darks were added to the slates in the paths to define them better, and Yellow Ochre was added to the border edges, with some medium-strength darks between the chives and other leaves. Light shadow was created using violet washed on to the path edges, the path and the squashes, and violet with a touch of Quinacridone Magenta on the chive flowers.

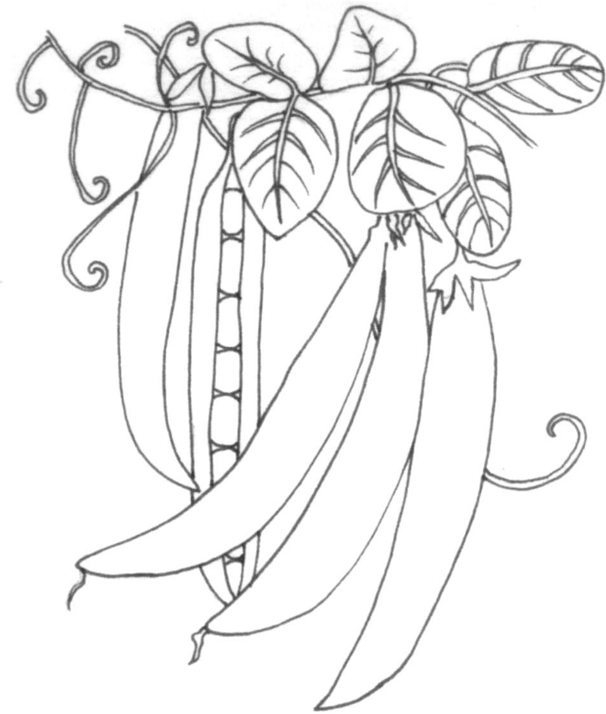

I regularly set the painting to view from a distance, sometimes returning to see it afresh, which allows me to decide if anything is needed. Perhaps I need to strengthen the darks, or blur edges, but invariably it is more darks that are needed.

The Gardener

Peas are my husband's favourite vegetable, so it is essential to grow plenty, though with staggered sowings as peas are best picked and eaten immediately for the sweetest flavour and before the sugars turn to starch. If they are to be frozen, it should be within a short time of picking. Seed catalogues describe peas as early, second earlies or maincrop, referring to their harvest time.

Peas have an extensive root run, so with wider spacing

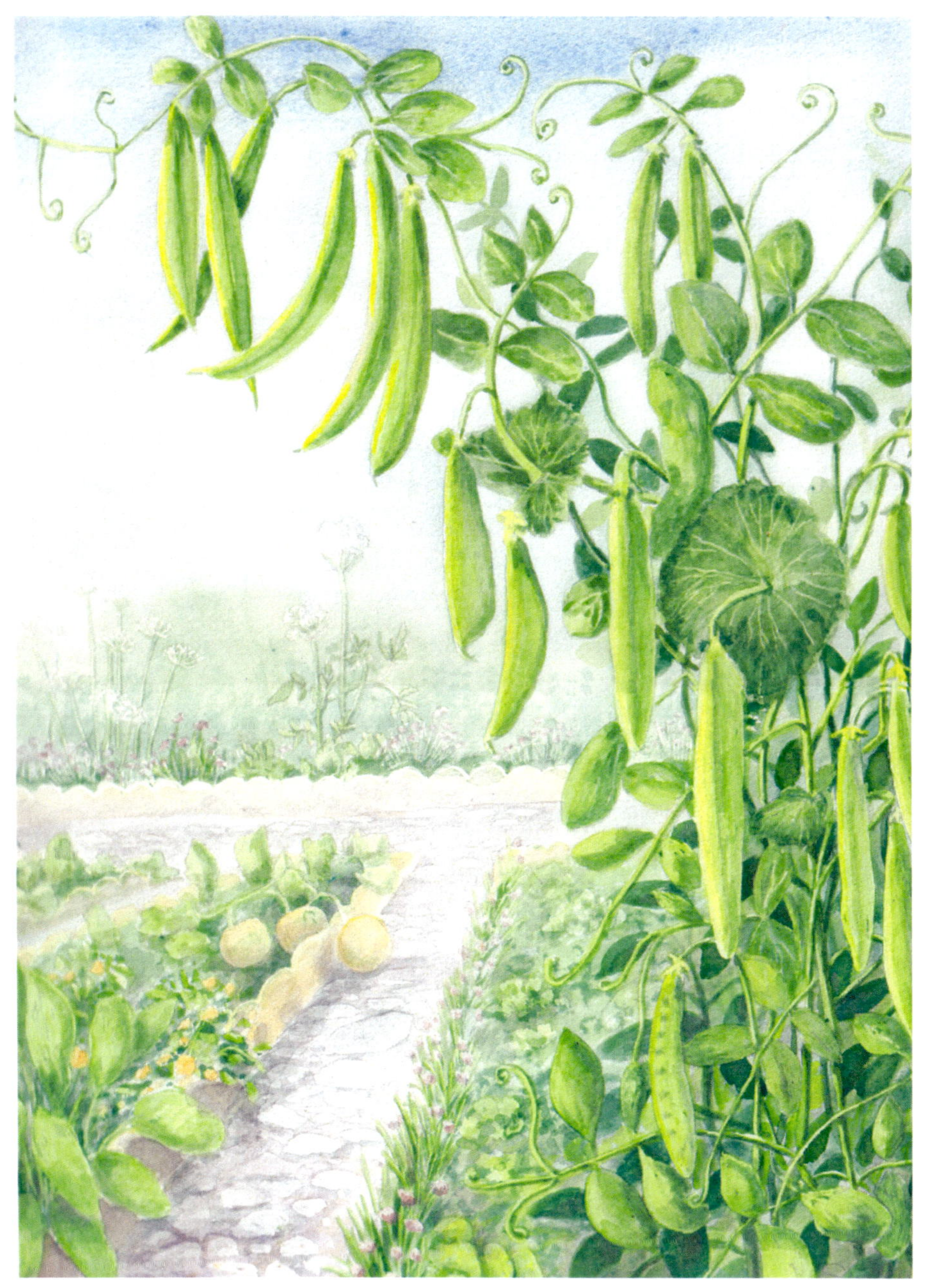

between seeds, a larger harvest is produced. The soil needs to be improved with well rotted compost or manure. This gives good drainage and retains moisture. Peas need plenty of water, so are best sown into a pre-wetted soil and left until the shoots appear before watering again. Overwatering can result in taller, thinner plants. They require more water when flowering so as to swell the pods to full capacity.

Seeds sown in a sunny site with later summer sowing are best in a cooler, shadier area. Sowing peas earlier in the year helps them to crop before the pea moths arrive in summer. Guttering is useful for sowing peas as the plantlets can be slid into a pre-dug trench. When the plantlets emerge, they are staked, usually with twigs and garden prunings, so that the peas' tendrils climb and attach for support.

Peas are in the legume family. They take nitrogen from the air, benefiting the pods of the plant via their roots; a follow-on crop of brassicas will benefit from the extra nitrogen. Mice and birds can be a problem, as they eat the seeds and emerging shoots. This happened last year to my autumn sowing of peas in the greenhouse – intended for harvesting in spring.

Peas are high in vitamins A, B1 and C, folate, iron and calcium, as well as being high in protein and fibre.

ONION

The Drawing

Many of the world's masterpieces were drawn with a quill pen dipped in bistre and fortified with light washes of the same ink or some other soluble earth colour. When using waterproof ink, washes of watercolour can be brushed over without fear of rubbing the image or causing it to

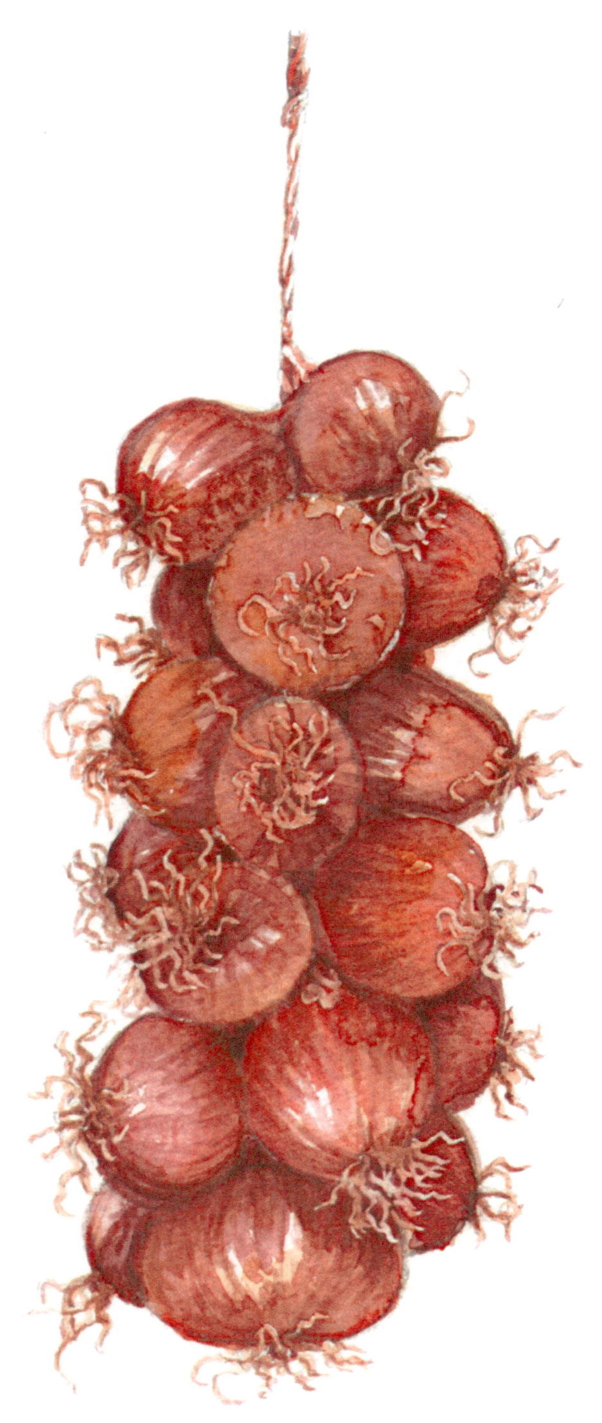

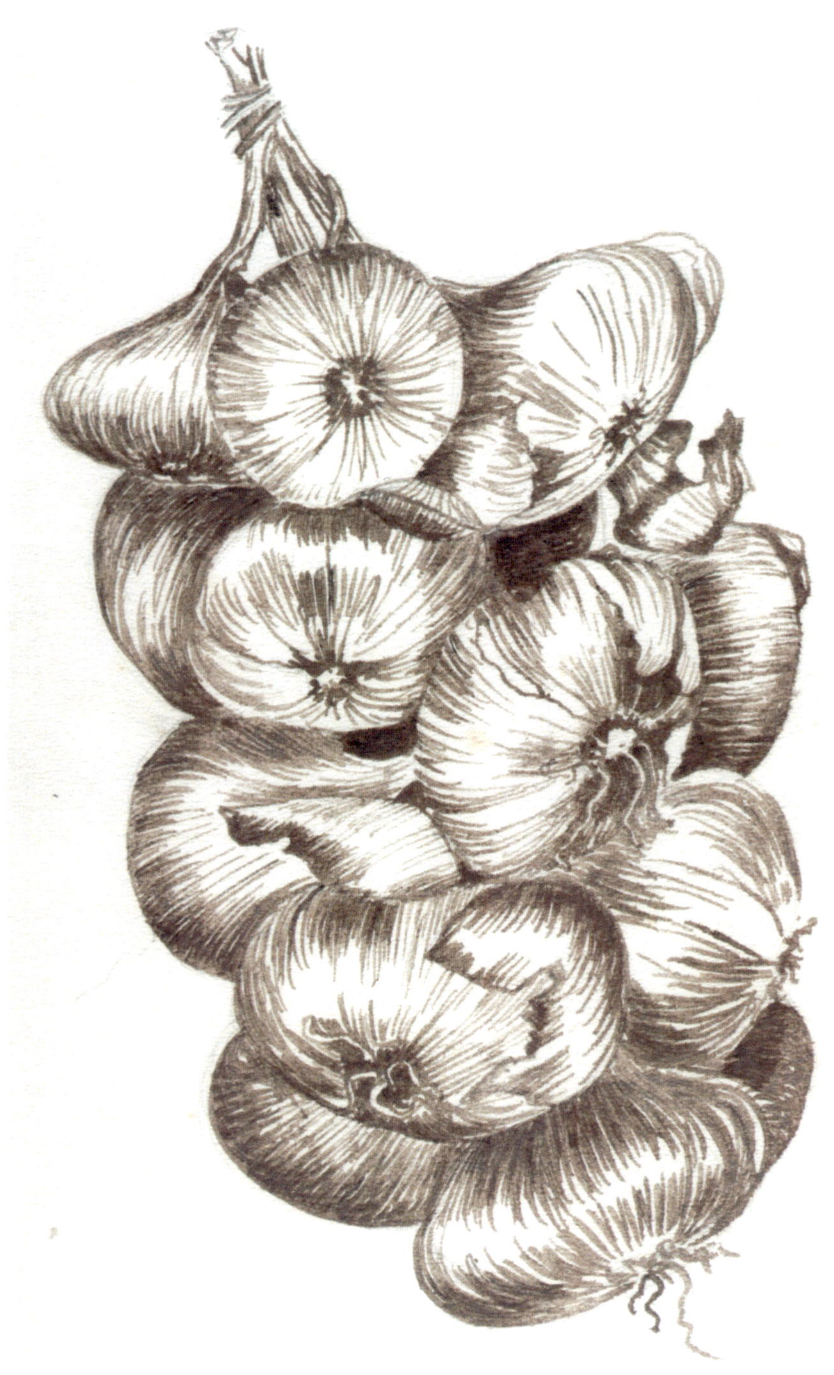

run. In this simple drawing of stringed onions on slightly textured paper, I used diluted ink to give some tone, using angled lines to give a textural effect.

The Painting

I first masked the roots of the onions before laying in watercolour washes of Mars Violet in the direction of the ridges on surfaces of the skins. I used a thick, round brush with short hairs to give a grainy look to the deepest darks. More layers were added enriching the hue and building up texture, leaving some unpainted areas for highlights, all the time thinking about how some shapes connect and relate to each other and some stand apart. Lastly the masking fluid was removed and the roots coloured with dilute paint.

The Gardener

The onion is one of the oldest cultivated vegetables, native to Asia but adopted and consequently associated with the Egyptians in design and religious belief. Onions have had a reputation of being difficult to cultivate, but modern varieties have been developed to suit most conditions. Soil preparation is important, done by adding as much manure and compost as possible. This is best done in the autumn, so that winter cold and rain settles the soil naturally. In early spring, the plot should be raked and firmed to a fine tilth. Onions can be grown in the same site each year, so long as the soil is enriched. Outdoor sowings can be made from early to late spring, so long as the weather is warm, sowing thinly and evenly in drills. If sown in autumn, the plants have a longer time of growth and will mature earlier than spring sowings. Later sowings will need cloche protection in winter. A late sowing will not mean late development, but smaller bulbs. The earlier the seeds are sown, the larger the bulbs. For larger bulbs, the seed can be sown in warmth, in late winter, hardened off, and planted out in late spring. Onion sets, or bulbs, can be purchased, and planted in drills just deep enough to cover the sets. Bulbs should be watered during dry spells.

When the leaves fall and discolour, the sap to the leaves is cut off, and eventually the leaves turn yellow and the stalks of the bulbs go brown. This means that the bulbs are ready to be harvested and should be lifted with a fork and spread out to dry, turning occasionally. Cloches can be useful to keep them dry with the open ends ensuring air flow. When the tops can be rubbed off they can be stored in a dry, airy place. A space-saving idea is to string the onions together and hang them instead of laying them in boxes.

The Welsh onion, *Allium fistulosum*, is believed to originate from Eastern Asia, but was known to the ancient world. The leaves are mild in flavour, similar to spring onions. The tree onion, *Allium cepa*, is a perennial, as are all the allium species, and develops a 'bulb' consisting of layers at the swollen stem base. This is protected by a skin that is impervious to water.

Apart from the onion's powerful aroma and flavour, which, when cooked, enhances all other flavours, the whole of the allium family contains phosphorus and sulphurous elements and has an ancient reputation for its cleansing properties. Culpeper said that 'Roasted under the embers and eaten with honey or sugar, they much conduce to relieve an inveterate cough and expectorate tough phlegm.' In the Middle Ages they were believed to draw putrefaction to them. One country practice remedy was to hollow out an onion, fill the centre with black treacle, roast the onion and, after removing the outer skin, mash the hot black paste for use as a poultice.

GARLIC

The Drawing

An artist will draw with anything and make it work to advantage – anything to be able to draw. A pencil is the simplest and most universal tool and is very versatile. Any decent cartridge paper is suitable. In this drawing of garlic, I used light-textured watercolour paper, which is evident in the grainy marks in the mid tones. I noted the whole basic shapes and drew in the outline simply and as accurately as possible with a B pencil, before breaking it into its component shapes and noting how each shape relates to its neighbour. Then I sketched in each shape with details of light and shade, building up the shadow and emphasising edges, but leaving blank paper to indicate where the light falls most brilliantly. The deepest dark was drawn with a 6B, which, with the firm pressure, was wonderfully black and filled the grain of the paper.

There is no substitute for clear observation, seeing the object for what it is rather than what is expected. Drawing with careful attention helps explain the marks made. These marks convince the eye, and hence the brain, into recognising images, by their texture. This can be difficult in a drawing because two dimensions are trying to indicate three. The flat paper surface has to appear as the shape projecting towards the viewer or receding, and marks indicating light and shade suggest the dimensional aspects of the form. The mind assembles these marks into an understanding of solidity as only solid objects can have some parts in light and other parts in shadow.

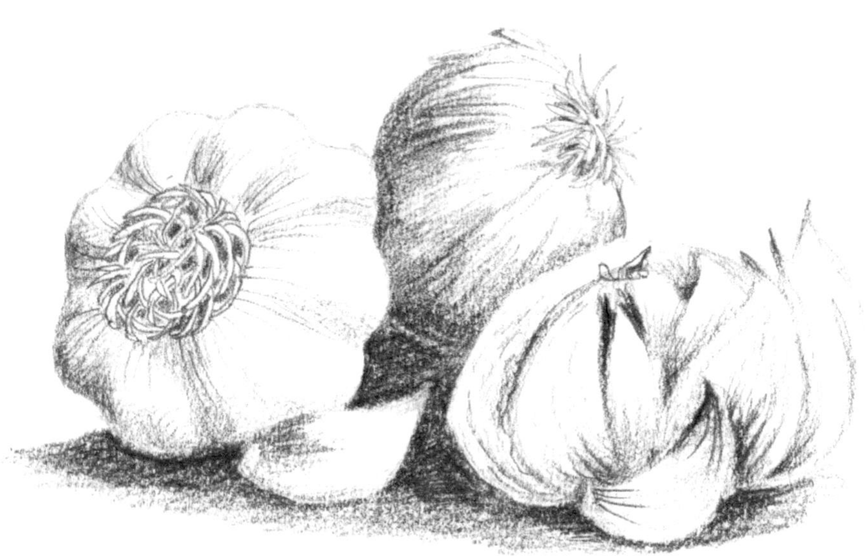

The Gardener

Garlic is high in amino acid allin, vitamins A and C, minerals manganese and calcium, supporting a defence against viral, bacterial and fungal infections, lowering the risk of heart disease and slowing the growth of cancer cells. Garlic is enormously beneficial for health and has been used for at least 5,000 years.

Garlic grows best in a sunny spot in rich soil with good drainage. Water during spring and summer and stop as soon as the leaves yellow or when they flop over, when they are ready to harvest. The cloves can be lifted and dried in the sun and then stored in a cool, dry place out of the sun. Avoid cold places, which encourage sprouting. If this happens, I plunge the sprouted garlic into water, wait several weeks, then strain and use the liquid as a garlic spray to deter aphids on roses.

GARLIC CHIVES

The Painting

This was painted on smooth Arches paper, leaving unpainted white paper for the flowers. I chose *Allium schoenoprasum* and *Allium neapolitanum* because I love the flowers. It was necessary to tone the inner white of the petals so as to give

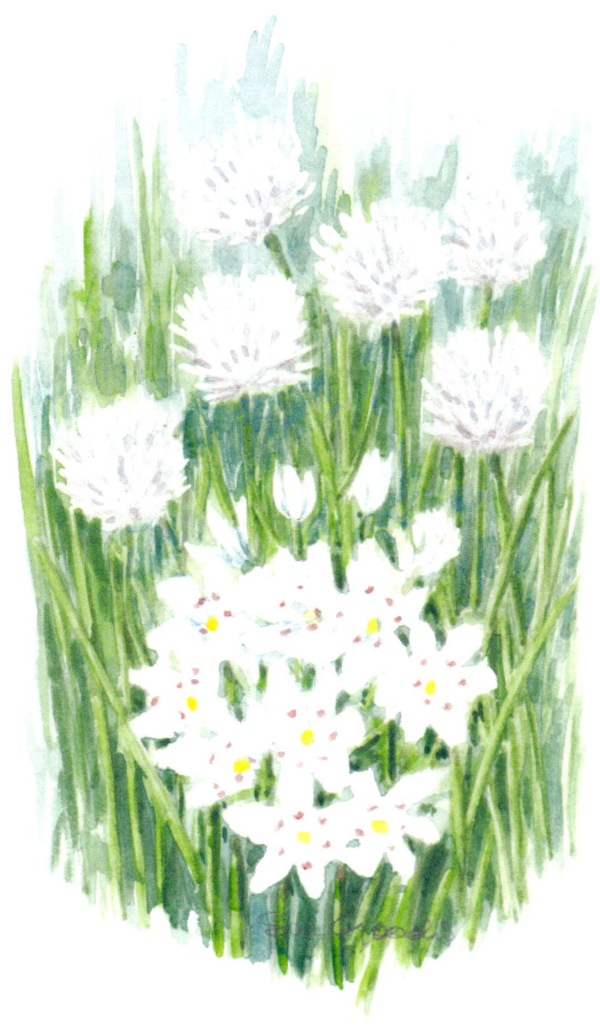

them shape and form. The same Cobalt Blue was used in the background and in mixing the green, along with Lemon Yellow darkened with Quinacridone Magenta for shadows and also in the stamens.

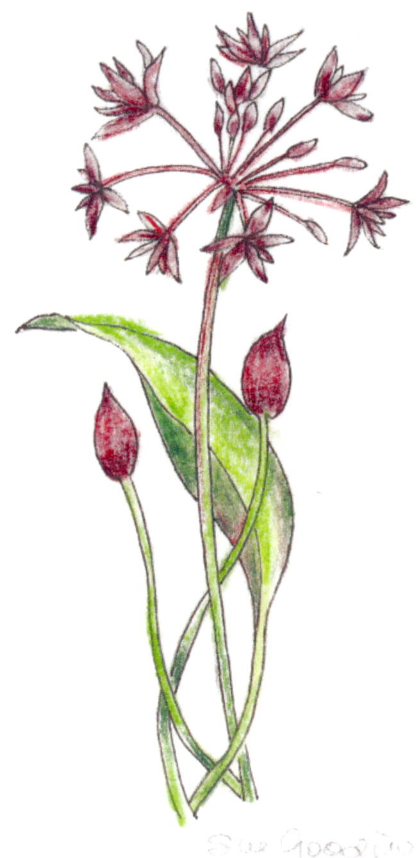

The Gardener

Garlic chives are more delicately flavoured than garlic. To propagate chives, the clumps of little bulblets can be divided after flowering, or increased by saving and sowing seed.

Wild garlic, or ramsons, is often detected by its smell long before it is in sight. Wild garlic has starry white flowers in summer. Country names abound: hog's garlick, buck rams, rams, ramaden, ramsey, rummy and stink plant.

Garlic mustard grows naturally on many continents. The flowers and leaves add a subtle flavour, while the root is hot and spicy, similar to horseradish.

ARTICHOKES

The Painting
Watercolour painting is a rich, spontaneous medium, providing a balance between masses of colour, and with the contrast of soft and sharp brushstrokes. Watercolour needs an understanding of basic truths and lots of practice. A wash of colour is painted using the minimum number of brushstrokes to achieve the desired value and colour.

I decided to use Sap Green for the central plant and darkened the side by mixing in Burnt Sienna. This was used for the shadows and underneath the foreground leaves. The background plants were painted with Hooker's Green and darkened with a little sienna. When all was dry, I wet the whole background using a large wash brush, but being very careful around the already painted leaves. Ultramarine Blue was washed into the top down into Phthalo Blue running down below the plants. More darks were added in the centre of the plant and shaded areas.

The marigold flowers were painted with Lemon yellow with their centres Sienna and a touch of Winsor Orange. The leaves of the marigolds are more of a yellow-green than those of the blue-green of the artichoke, helping to give an impression of size and depth, with the yellow coming forward and the blue receding.

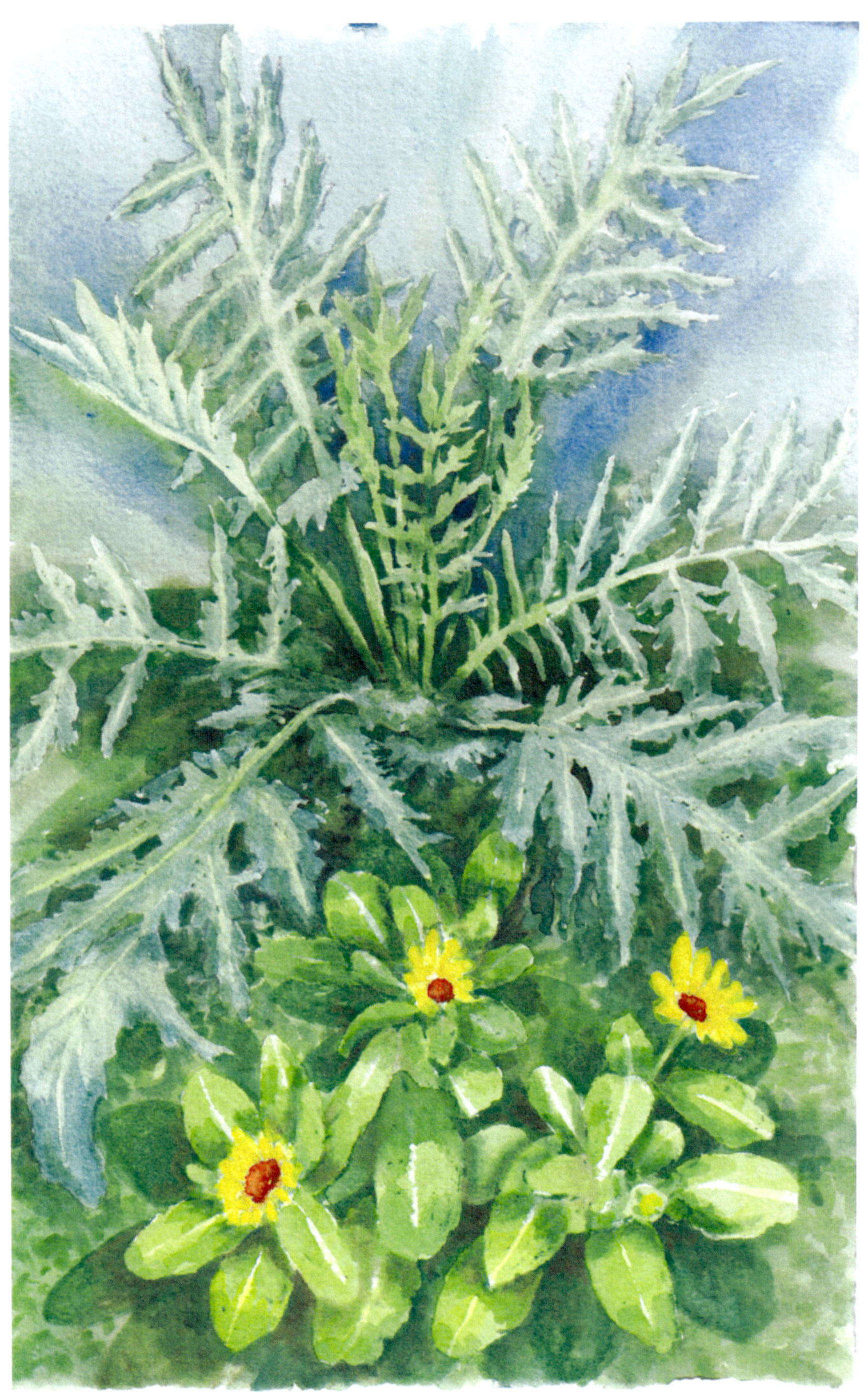

The Gardener

I adore the fabulous architectural foliage and grow artichokes as decorative plants as well as for harvesting the chokes, which are also beautiful if left to flower. Artichokes are perennial and grow easily from seed in spring, planted out in summer. They produce very large plants. They like a rich, well-drained soil in full sun. They are not very hardy and the wind is a problem as it catches their large leaves, tearing them at the base. However, they soon grow more leaves from the centre and recover well. Shelter from hedges and shrubs can filter the wind, creating a microclimate within the garden so that tender plants can be protected. Cold weather can be a positive control against pests and diseases.

In the following spring the plants produce chokes which can be cut when small, fried and served with butter. The larger chokes can be boiled and eaten with oil and butter. I prefer to leave them to develop their beautiful, purple, structural flowering heads, just as any herbaceous perennial. Artichokes provide graceful, silvery accent in the borders blessed with fabulous flowers.

Offsets from the mature plants can provide new plants which produce chokes in their second or third year. These will establish more quickly than sowing seed. They are not frost-hardy, so need winter protection.

I encourage marigolds into the vegetable garden as they deter certain unwanted insects. They self seed but are easy to control and bring a welcome burst of colour even in winter.

JERUSALEM ARTICHOKE

The Painting

I wanted to use a simple palette of blues and yellows. By using yellow as a high key, a cheerful mood is suggested, allowing one colour to dominate – a technique exploited by artists from Van Gogh onwards. I started with a base Lemon Yellow for the flower petals, then, when dry, wet around the petals with clear water and dropped in various blues at random in the sky area and a few areas of yellow in the background, interspersed with green mixed from the two colours. The foreground leaves and stalks were depicted carefully, with those behind suggested (rather than accurately drawn) using a large brush and several greens. It can be challenging to simplify, but worth doing to express emotional and atmospheric elements. With the subject being so intricate and complex, there is a temptation to paint every aspect in detail rather than to simplify and to let the brushstrokes suggest elements and stimulate the imagination. Simplification is leaving out some details, painting lost and found edges where the tones and colours of an object and its background are subtly implied, giving an illusion of reality.

Various greens were added, gradually darkening behind the main subjects. I then added Indian Yellow to the petals and Burnt Sienna to the flower centres, darkening with Phthalo Blue. The shadows had to be painted delicately so as not to muddy the yellow. For this I used Yellow Ochre. More lemon was added to the foliage both in the foreground and mid distance, and dark green for shadows. More blue was dabbed into the distant trees to give a feel of atmosphere, to complement the yellow and act as a link between the yellow and blue.

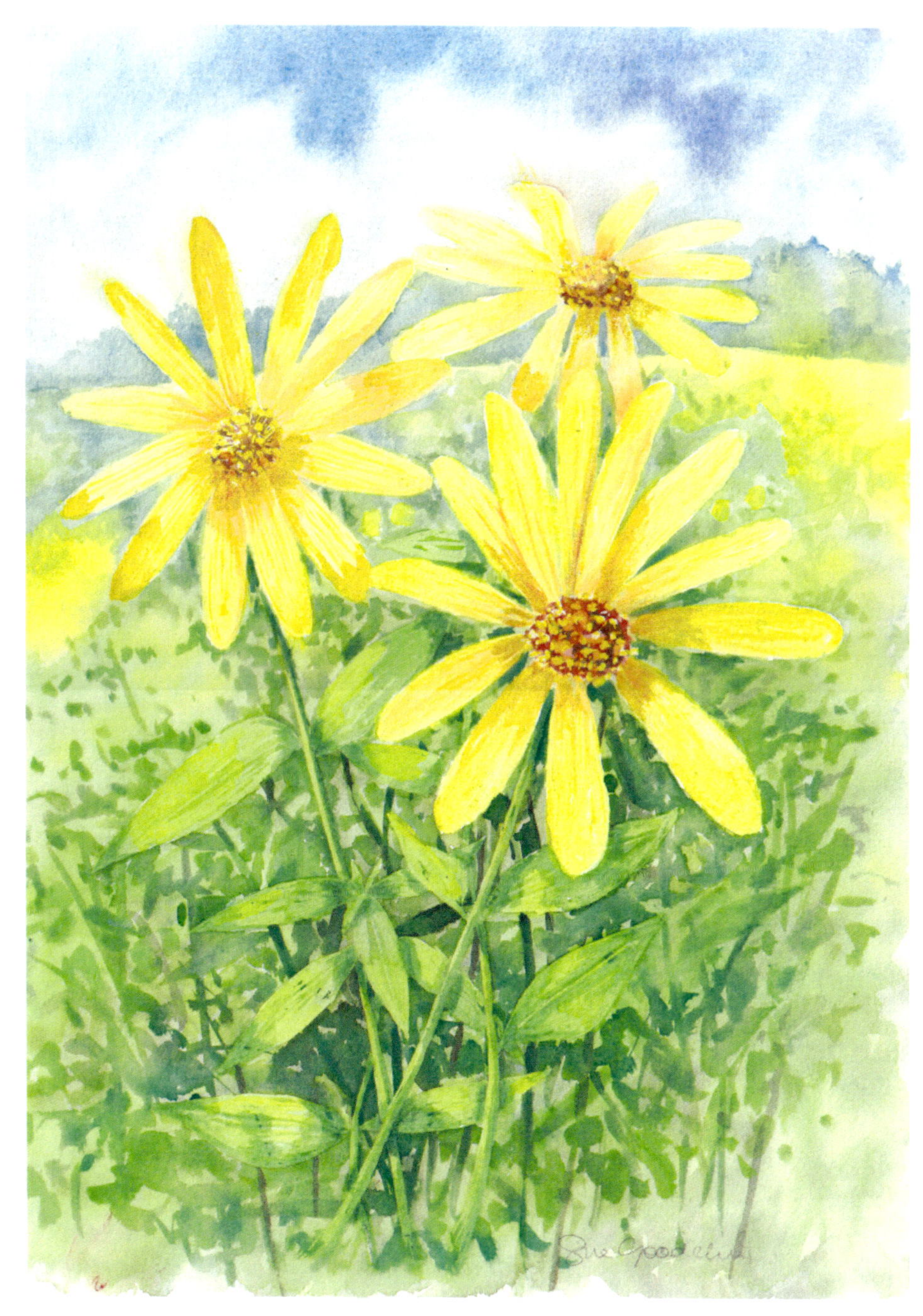

The Gardener

The tall Jerusalem artichoke, *Helianthus tuberosus*, is also known as sun-root, sun-choke and earth apple. In France it is called *topinambour*, which is also a term used for an uncouth, uneducated person. It is a species of sunflower from eastern North America, where it was a food crop. It can grow from one and a half to three metres tall, forming a beautiful screen giving protection to other plants which don't particularly like our hot, dry summers. It helps to lower blood pressure, is high in potassium, decreases blood cholesterol, and is high in iron and protein. It is often recommended as a potato substitute for diabetics.

Sir Walter Raleigh found native Americans cultivating the tubers in Virginia in 1585. In Europe it became known as Canadian or French potato. It is well suited to the European climate and consequently multiplies quickly, now being much more extensively cultivated in Europe than in America. In France, along with swedes, they became the most prevalent vegetable in World War II, giving it the reputation of a poor man's vegetable. The tubers persist in the ground for years. They can be eaten raw and are used as a source of fructose and to make alcohol.

Their inulin forms a carbohydrate which cannot be broken down by the human digestive system and causes flatulence. Even so, I appreciate the beautiful flowers.

Despite its name, it has no relationship to Jerusalem and is not an artichoke. It may be that it is a corruption of the Italian name *girasol*e, meaning sunflower, and the name artichoke comes from the taste of the edible tuber being similar to artichoke.

TOMATOES

The Painting

A choice of reds painted in the form of individual tomatoes gave the tonal range to suggest three-dimensional fruits. I started with fruits that didn't touch so that the washes stayed separate. For example, the top-left and top-right tomatoes and the second down the stalk on the left were painted leaving unpainted areas to represent shine. When dry, the other fruits were painted in the same way. The washes were initially Quinacridone Red Orange, Quinacridone Red, and Permanent Rose with Rose Madder Alizarin added into the darker, shaded sides. When dry, shaded areas were dampened and deeper colour added with touches of Ultramarine Violet. The lowest fruit was painted in the same way with Raw Sienna and a little Permanent Rose and then shadowed with a thin, diluted, violet.

The stem and hulls were painted with Sap Green darkened with violet.

The Gardener

Cherry tomatoes are rich in vitamin C, which is higher in smaller tomatoes. They are also high in fibre, potassium and folic acid. Tomatoes get their red colour from disease-fighting lycopene, which is released on cooking. Research has found that bright-orange tomatoes contain a different form of lycopene that is easier to absorb. The taste and smell of home-grown tomatoes is very special.

Some seeds can be sown directly into the ground while those that are tender such as tomatoes, peppers and cosmos, are best started indoors where it is easier to control conditions needed for germination. Most seeds

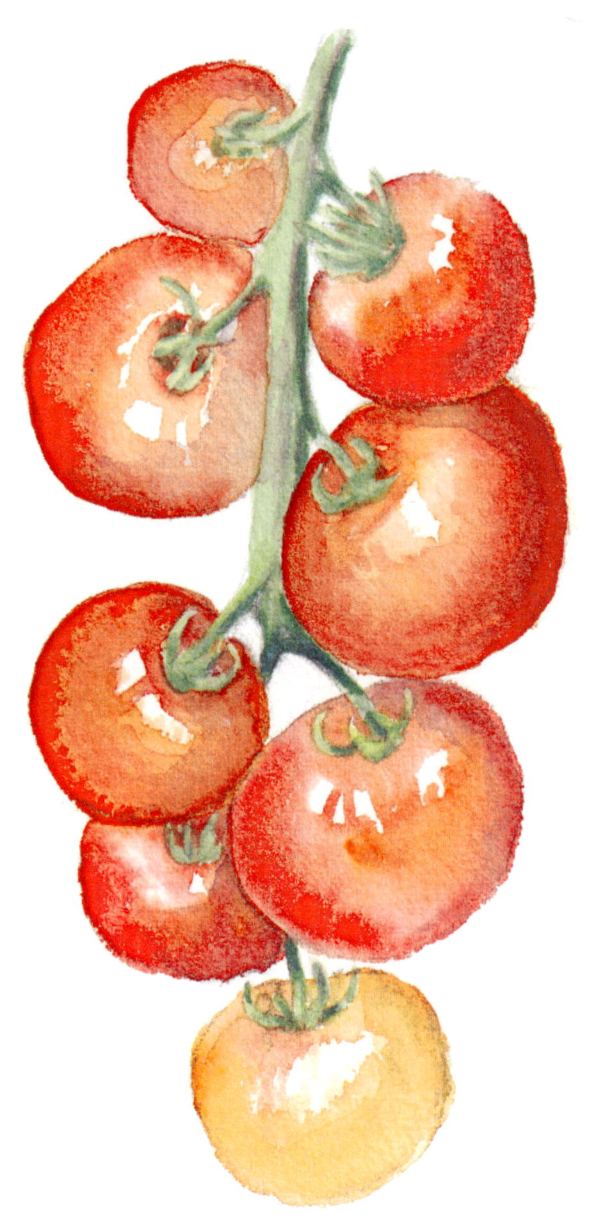

need plenty of light to germinate and some need extra heat from a propagator, which can begin early in the year using good-quality compost, though I usually find self-sown plants in the garden as they do very well in our mild climate. They are hungry feeders. Water the pots and press the seed into the compost and place them in good light. When large enough the seedlings can be pricked out, potted and eventually planted out. When pricking out, they should be lifted out of the pots by holding the leaf and not the stem, which can bruise. The young plants should then be grown on in warmth, planting deeply up to the first leaves. This encourages extra roots, helping the plant to take up more moisture. Tomato plants can be very delicate and for the first few weeks of growth they need warmth, care and attention. The more space they have, the stronger they will be. This gives the plant the best chance to grow well. If grown on in the garden, the ground should be well cultivated prior to planting. I place a cane beside each plant and tie it to the cane. Tomatoes grow quickly, so need training every few days; otherwise they outgrow their supports.

Commercial growers feed their plants with nitrogen so as to produce a heavy yield, but with a loss of flavour. I prefer to feed them with my own home-made comfrey mix, which is potassium-rich and encourages flowering rather than growth, producing a moderate crop from each plant rich in flavour and sweetness. If the tips of the plant are pinched off after four or five trusses have formed, the plant's energy is concentrated into swelling and ripening the fruit.

Alternately soaking the soil and letting it dry out is a bad idea as it encourages blossom-end rot. This is when the end furthest away from the stalk becomes flattened and turns dark brown or black. But, kept fed and watered, tomatoes will continue to produce fruit into autumn.

Ripening depends on the temperature, and the leaves do not need to be stripped off as they are a valuable food manufacturer. Only yellow leaves need to be removed. Bush tomatoes do not need side shoots removing.

Aphids prefer lush green foliage but dislike aromatic plants, so growing plants like tagetes, mint and basil among the tomatoes can deter whitefly. Similarly the scent of tomatoes grown among brassicas can repel butterflies, and hence caterpillars.

BROAD BEANS

The Painting

This started as a pencil drawing with various greens added – Sap Green, Hooker's Green – with Burnt Umber added to darken the tone. These beans were drawn from life and then rearranged from the sketchbook when in the studio. I had noted the natural habit of the plant, which meant that the composition was arranged sympathetically. It is important for a natural look to have some stems overlapping or crossing or sideways, as they were in the garden.

Watercolour dries paler, so I try to achieve a deeper colour right from the start, but sometimes more colour is needed later. In this case, I painted over with Lemon Yellow in places, just to brighten the greens. This is why it is important to step back to look at the painting and assess it – sometimes looking at it in reverse in a mirror helps to show any imbalance.

The Gardener

Broad beans are a very old and easily cultivated vegetable with a history dating back thousands of years, being the staple diet for the many countries in medieval Western Asia, the

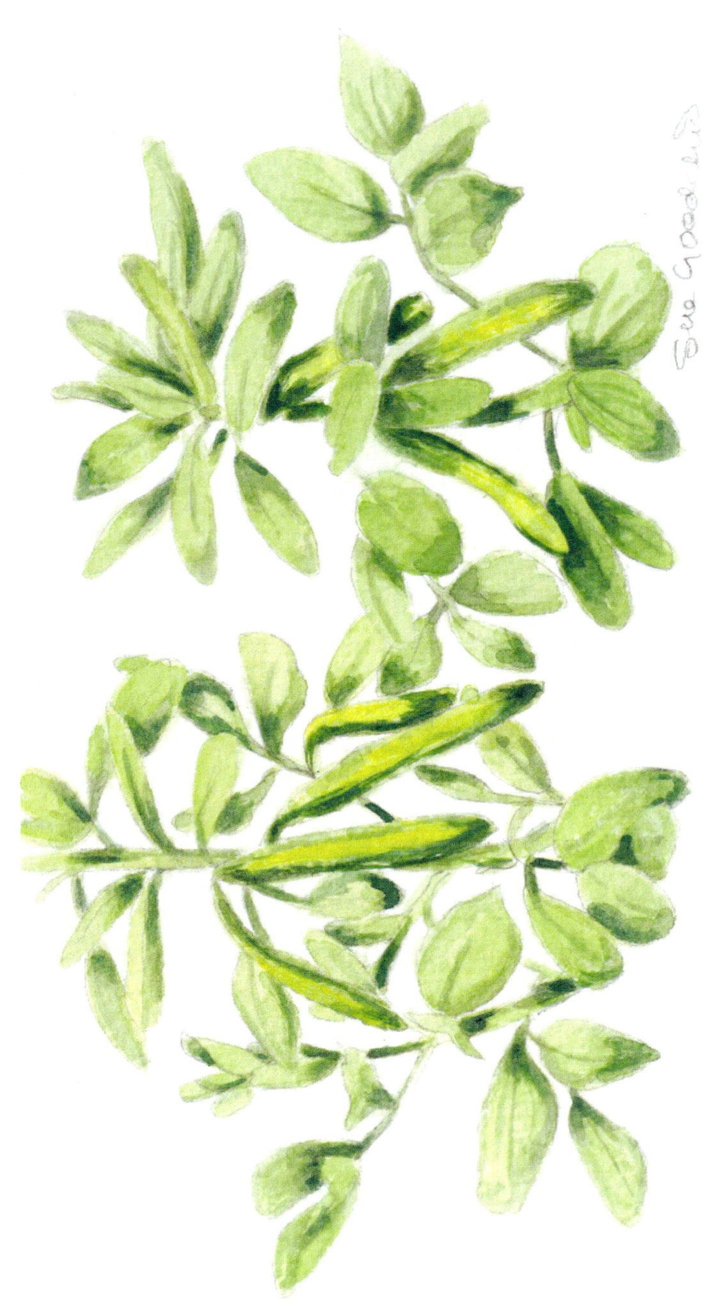

Mediterranean and Northern Europe. Even today, each year's new crop causes great excitement in rural communities. The sage Greek philosopher Pythagoras supposedly banned the eating of broad beans because they contained the souls of the dead.

Early sowings in October give a harvest in May or June, and sowing later for autumn harvests ensures tender beans so long as they are harvested when young, sweet and small. When the plants are in full flower, I pinch out the top shoot to reduce the danger of black aphid attacking and feeding on the young shoots and to encourage a more uniform development of pods. Broad beans are best picked young, shelled and cooked whole. The plants need support with canes and string to support them when windy.

They have very long roots which allow them to access minerals which shallow rooted plants cannot reach. After harvesting, the top of the plant can be cut off and composted and the roots dug into the ground. This improves the soil fertility because, as with all legumes, broad beans fix nitrogen from the air into the soil via their root nodules and hence are an excellent fertiliser for the following crop. Nitrogen is essential for green growth. Too much encourages lush growth with fewer flowers and pods, but too little will result in slow growth and yellowing leaves. To encourage flowering, potassium is essential. This is found in wood ash, blood, fish and bone, seaweed, hoof and horn and home-made compost. I make a liquid potash fertiliser by steeping comfrey in water for several weeks. Phosphorus is needed for strong roots and germination. Chicken manure is high in nitrogen, phosphates, sulphur, magnesium and lime and, along with horse manure, which is high in nitrogen, is ideal for lightening the soil texture and increasing the heat in the compost heap, speeding decompostion.

CARROT

The Drawing

A drawing in ink. I decided it would be better to show the harvested roots as a bunch, interesting as they interlocked one behind another and the feathery foliage created a pattern. Ink pens can be less expressive than a brush or dip pen, producing hard, solid, quick marks which have to be used carefully when precision is required. The tight lines of the roots contrast well with the looser, more fluid marks of the feathery leaves of the carrot tops.

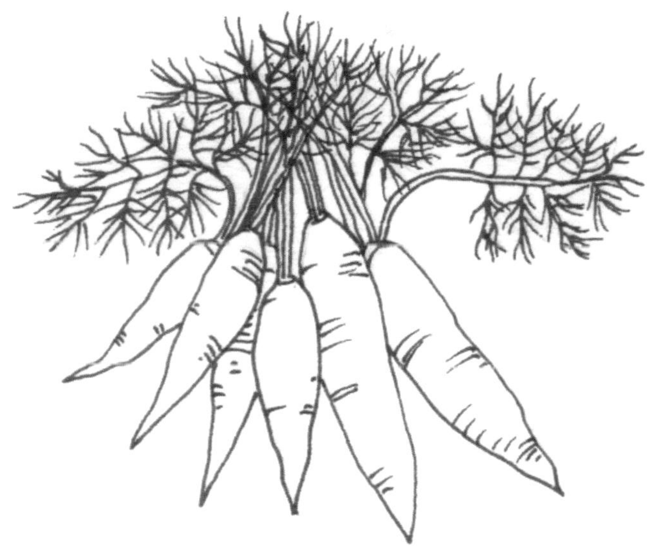

The Gardener

A fine excuse to use the bright colours of orange, yellow and red. I first washed the watercolour paper with concentrated Winsor Orange, a semi-opaque colour but has excellent mixing qualities. Into this, whilst still wet, Indian Yellow, a warm yellow, was added so that they merged. When dry each individual carrot was edged with these same colours plus Quinacridone Red, a dark, transparent red with a touch of violet. Quinacridone colours are organic compounds with exceptional colour and light-fastness. They supplant many fugitive paints. The shine on the centres of the carrots where the light caught them, was lifted out using a damp flat brush, wiping the colour onto a tissue each time before lifting out another shine. Shadows on the sides of the carrots and the background was Quinacidone Violet, which appeared more red when painted over the orange underpainting. The few leaves were painted with Sap Green, a bright yellowy-green which contrasted well with the colours of the roots.

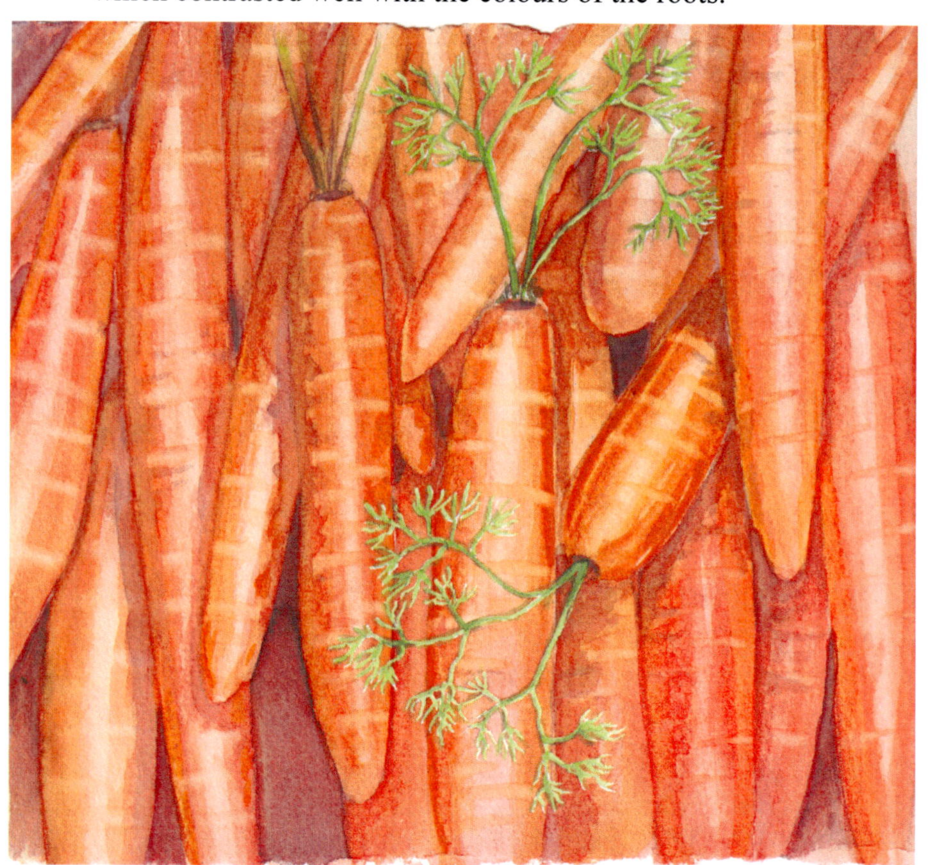

The Gardener

Carrots are highly nutritious being rich in vitamin A.

Seed can be sown in early spring when the ground has warmed, preferably in full sun. When sowing I mix the seeds with sand, which helps to sow them thinly as thinning could attract the carrot fly. Carrots will grow long and straight if sown into deeply dug soil manured for a previous crop or dug over in the autumn and left rough for the winter weather to break it down to a fine structure. If they are grown on new manure they will grow forked and tangled. If grown in poor soil they will be weak, and they do not like being transplanted. Just as with parsnips, the deeper the topsoil the better the roots of carrots can grow, take up nutrients and retain water. It also means that the soil has a high level of bacterial activity, which is good for all-round health.

There are many varieties – maincrop, stump, long and intermediate rooted.

Vegetables such as carrots, parsley and beetroot, which are biennial, grow roots in their first year and flowers in the second. If allowed to set seed, rather than being harvested, their flowers will attract beneficial insects, such as hoverflies and lacewings,which help to control pests like aphids and in turn protect other plants. The aroma of sage repels moths, ants, slugs, carrot flies and cabbage moths, as can garlic or chives. By not clearing the plot until spring, the dry top growth provides shelter for newly emerging plants and cover for insects and birds, which will eat seeds and berries.

Wild carrots have white roots, though there are purple, violet and yellow. The man-made orange carrot was bred by the Dutch in the eighteenth century.

POTATOES

The Drawing

There's something magical about holding a pencil. I feel that the pencil is the most expressive, versatile and economic tool, and the most neglected. Artists are, of course, particularly familiar with the pencil for preliminary studies and sketches. Few regard it as a medium in itself. As a student, I loved the drawing lessons, mostly involving subjects in the Natural History Museum, while the other students wanted colour and immediate impact. With creative handling, the graphite pencil can produce more varied effects than any other black and white medium. Drawing with shades of black-and-white trains the artist to concentrate on tonal values. One of the advantages of the pencil is that it can be used in so many different ways, by sharpening the lead point differently, producing distinctively drawn lines. The various grades of lead, from very hard to very soft, produce variety in tone and line. The pencil is classified according to degrees of hardness or softness. All degrees are useful, but, for sketching, the softer varieties are better as they glide over the surface of the paper and make a more responsive line. Softer pencils are good for shadows; hard varieties are good for careful outline studies and meticulous work. Pencil is also compatible with a wide variety of paper surfaces, whose textures can add a great deal of interest to a drawing.

The pencil is inseparable from art, since most paintings, ink drawings, illustrations, lithographs, engravings and sculpture begin as pencil drawings. It is also well suited for highly finished drawings that are an end in themselves. Few artists develop their pencil-drawing techniques because the pencil is most often used for preliminary work and sketches.

These potatoes were outlined and the light and shade noted. The lightest tone was against the darkest tone and I also noted some reflected light from the surface, which gave a sense of volume. Light against dark helps to give a sense of depth. Where the shading is light the grain of the paper is visible but not in the deepest darks, where more pressure has been used.

If handled with care, pencil drawings will not smudge, but it is safer to spray them with fixative. The drawing should be horizontal while being sprayed with a light coat, and allowed to dry before applying a second or third coat.

The spontaneity and freedom one gets when drawing

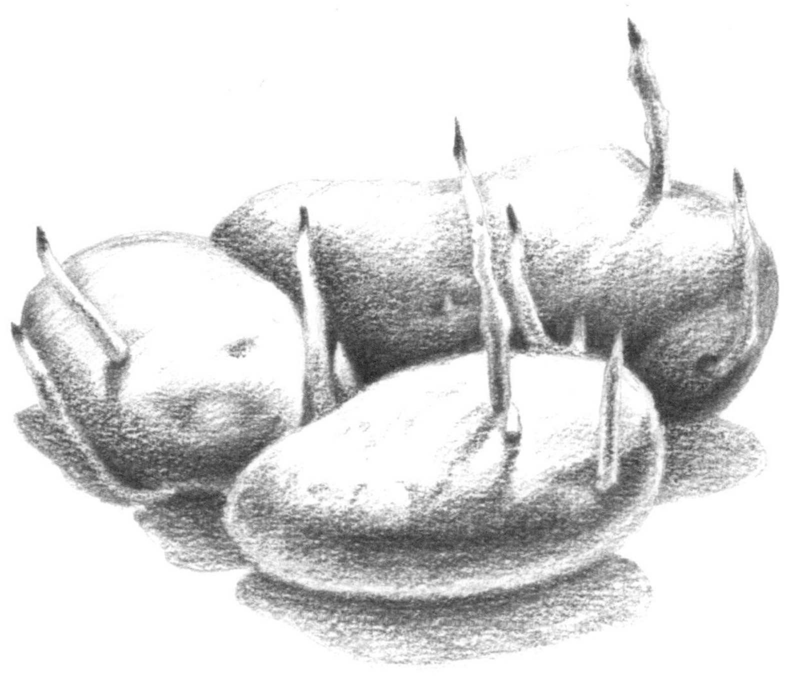

directly from nature is worth any problems encountered.

The Gardener
The potato is a perennial from South America, called 'skyrrets of Peru'. A potato tuber is an underground stem, modified as a food-storage organ. Although called 'seed' potatoes, they are in fact tubers. A potato tuber is marked by a scar at one end, where it was attached to the parent plant, and by 'eyes', or 'nodes', around the surface. It is these that make roots and shoots, establishing a new plant. They can be chitted. This means exposing them to light so that they develop shoots before they are planted with the 'eye' uppermost. This may take several weeks, depending on the variety. The trench method is the traditional way of planting potatoes. The tubers are planted at the bottom of a trench and this is filled in from a second trench.

Once the leaves have formed, the potatoes are 'earthed up' with a hoe, being careful so as not to cut off the underground stolons. This ridge prevents the tubers pushing up into the sunlight and turning green and poisonous. They are best watered when they flower as this dramatically increases the crop.

Early potatoes should be ready to harvest in June or July, and used straight away. Seconds and main crops are harvested from August onwards when the tops have died down. Dry them in the sun for a few hours before storing in boxes in an airy place away from the light. They can be left in the ground unharvested for at least a month, but taste best when cooked straight away.

SWEET POTATO

The Painting

It was quite difficult to become enthusiastic about painting roots, so I decided to paint the whole plant, showing the shape of the roots and their attractive colour. After all, it was fun painting the roots with Ultramarine Violet run into Quinacridone Magenta; and whilst the paint was still wet, I ran Winsor Orange into their centres so that the colours merged. The background was painted loosely using a large brush in both cool and warm greens, as opposed to the bright

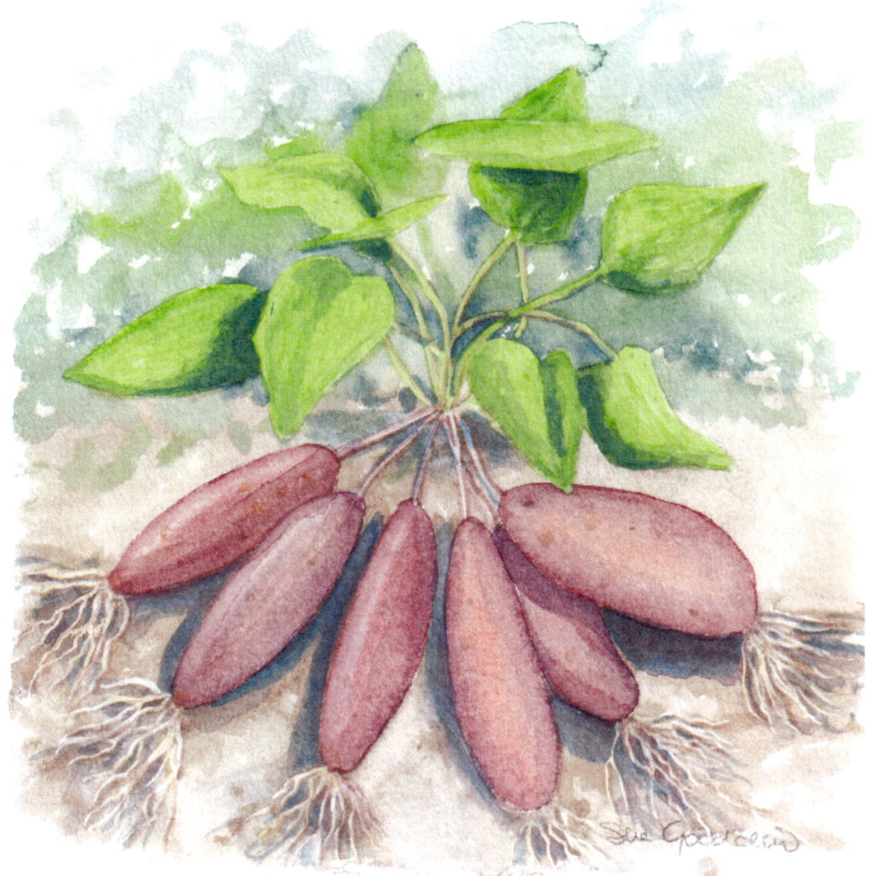

green of the sweet-potato leaves. The foreground was equally loosely painted, with Burnt Umber. Watercolour is painted from light to dark. Dark areas can be washed over and more darks added if needed.

The Gardener

The sweet potato belongs to the bindweed or morning-glory family, *Convolvulaceae*. It has large, starchy, sweet tasting tuberous roots which are an excellent source of vitamins A (in the form of beta-carotene), C, B1, B2 and B6, manganese, copper, pantothenic acid, potassium, niacin, phosphorus and dietary fibre. The young leaves can be eaten as greens. As I grow my own and they are not treated, I can eat the entire tuber, flesh and skin. It has been shown that boiling them has a more favourable impact on blood sugar.

There are about 400 varieties, with orange most common, also red, pink and some white, cream and yellow, these being less sweet. They are not started by seed, as with most vegetables, but from slips which grow from the tuber. They need warmth, and in a few weeks the tuber produces leafy sprouts and roots on the bottom. The slips should be planted in loose soil and watered every day for the first week. Harvest when the leaves start to yellow, but the longer the crop is left in the ground, the higher the yield and vitamin content. Care should be taken to avoid damage to the tender tubers. They should be stored in a cool, dark and well-ventilated place.

They are not frost-hardy as they are native to Central and South America. They are one of the oldest vegetables known to prehistoric man, relics having been found in Peruvian caves dating back to 8000 BC. Christopher Columbus brought the sweet potato back to Europe in 1492. Worldwide, about 80 million tons are grown in China, 14 million in Africa, two million in Central and South America and one million in US.

BEETROOT

The Drawing

I first cleaned the roots of mud and twisted off the foliage. I drew each root separately in ink, and made a design of them, placing them so that each one enhanced the others. The first coloured pencil was Madder Carmine applied with light pressure over all except for the shine, where the light hit their centres. I worked outwards to the edges, where more pressure deposited more pigment, giving a deeper,

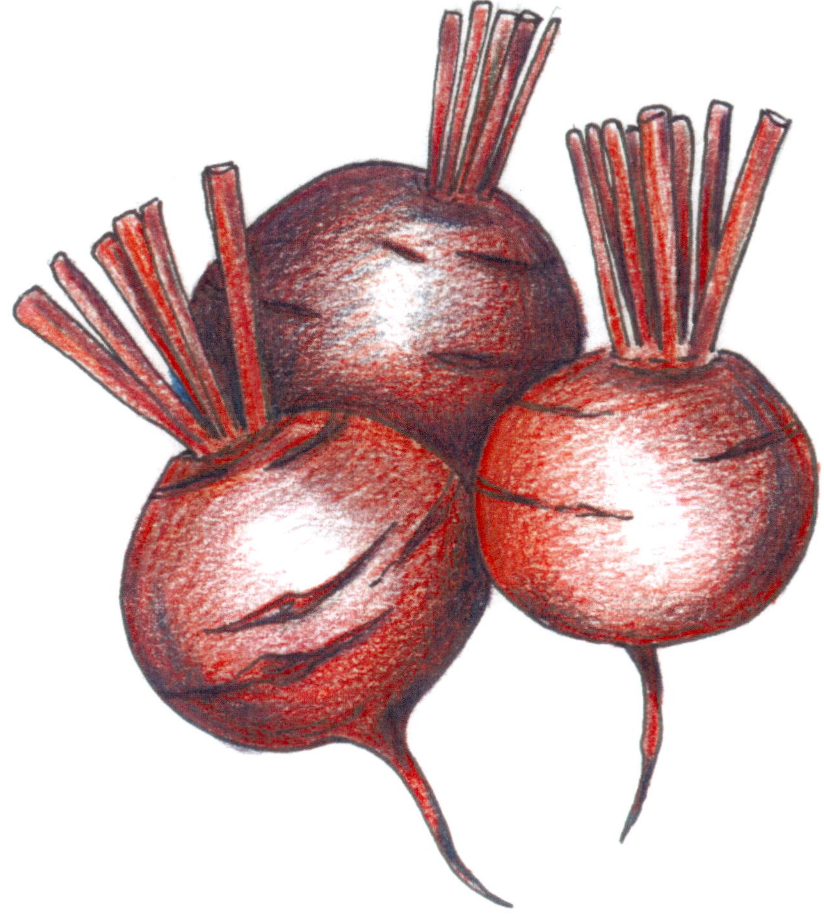

darker colour. Geranium Lake and Scarlet Lake were hatched over the Madder. Hatching is a tonal or shading effect using closely spaced parallel or crossed lines. This creates blocks of colour and tone, and different effects are produced by varying the thickness of the lines and spaces between them. Darks were added with Red Violet Lake hatched with Dark Violet. I placed the darkest darks beside the lighter foreground beetroots for maximum impact – the background beetroot was darker, helping to highlight areas of the foreground beets. A little Orange Chrome was added here and there.

Using only one colour can be limiting, but by choosing bright, saturated colours a wider range of hues develops. These layered colours interact visually, producing exciting and convincing seemingly three-dimensional drawings.

The Gardener

Beetroots are biennial plants grown for their swollen roots. They usually have red flesh, but can be pink and white ringed with golden leaves and roots. There is an unusual white beetroot called 'Detroit White', which has a delicate flavour and no stain. Beetroot can be round or long and tapering, the globe beetroot being the most popular. The cylindrical variety is bigger but grows more slowly, so is more suitable for maincrop use.

Care should be taken when sowing as the 'seed capsule' contains several seeds. They grow best in well-drained conditions in moisture-retentive compost, preferable in ground enriched for a previous crop. They do not germinate below 7°C, so need warm weather. Early crops can be sown in February in a cold frame or under cloches. Before sowing, water the drill and cover with dry soil as this suppresses the moisture long enough for germination. Beetroot is in season from May and throughout the winter. Slugs can be a problem, attacking the beetroot root as well as the young seedlings. The leaves are more nutritious than the root, being high in vitamin A, C, K, iron, magnesium, potassium and calcium. They contain high levels of nitrates, which improve blood health and help to lower blood pressure. The leaves are best eaten raw in salads or lightly cooked.

COURGETTES

The Painting

Watercolour is one of the most exciting expressive mediums. Painting and drawing with watercolour is not only a challenge, but enormous fun and can be an all-consuming passion. An image of striking simplicity is achieved by focusing on a single subject and handling it with confidence. Working with a variety of colours can be exciting; but equally, using a limited palette can be invigorating. Here I used the complementary colours of blue and yellow, with the blue next to the yellow making the yellow appear much brighter as well as giving a sense of depth to the painting.

The fluidity of the watercolour washes gives a sense of solid form with the colours fusing in places and stunningly sharp and contrasted in others. The most effective way of creating pure, sparkling highlights is to reserve any areas, and this must be planned in advance. A resist was drawn over the leaf veins so that a dark wash could be painted over it. When the resist was removed, the revealed white paper was toned with a yellowy green. As I painted, I

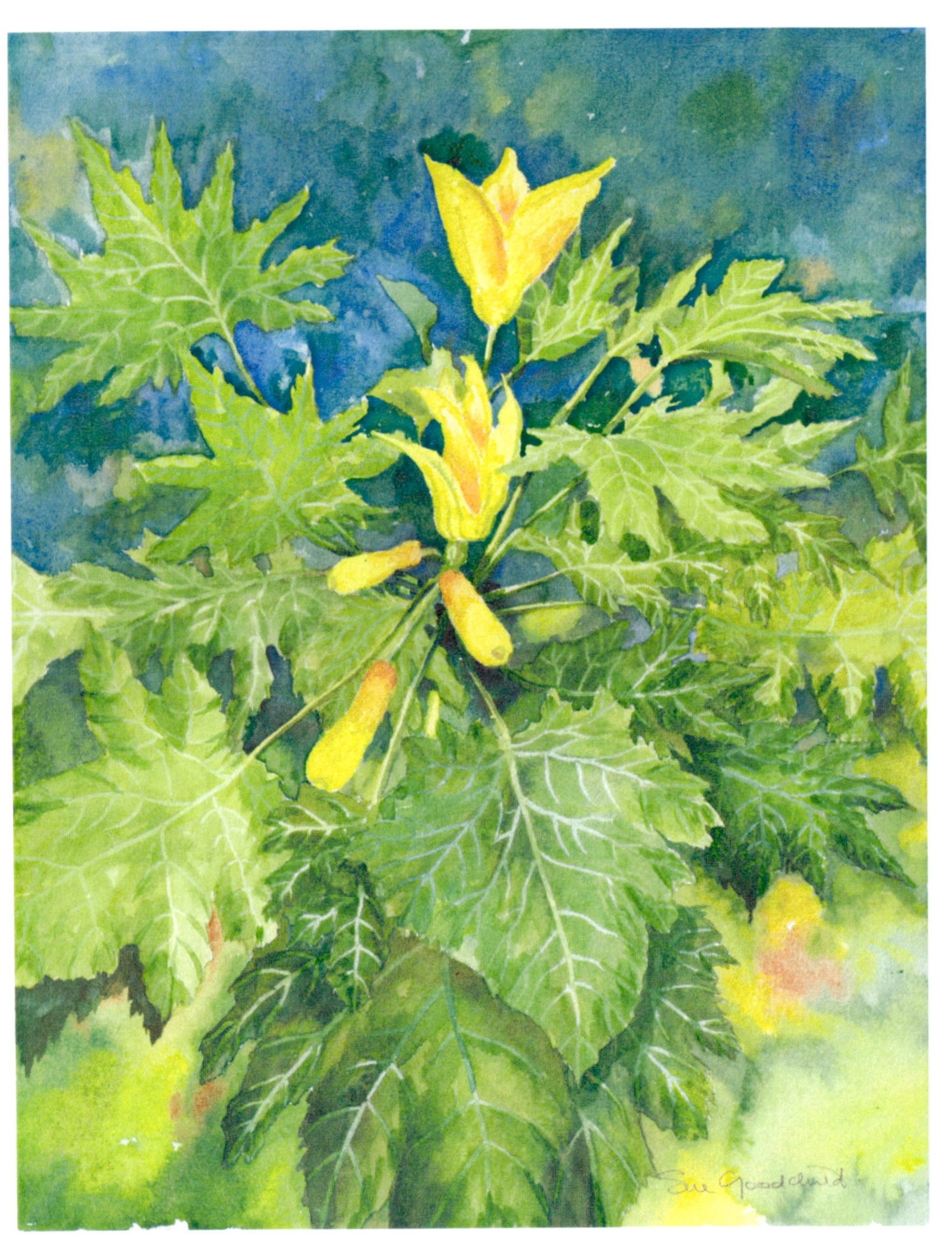
Sue Goodchild

was careful to check the relationship between the greens, mixing stonger greens in shadowed areas. When mixing greens, it is important to choose the right pigments. I mostly use Ultramarine Blue, which mixes well with other colours without dominating, whereas Phthalo Blue has more depth and saturation and when mixed with other colours can take over.

The Gardener

I prepare the soil in the winter, enriching it with manure and compost. The large courgette seeds are best planted in individual modules filled with compost, placed on their side because if flat, water may remain on their surface and cause rot. The seeds can be placed in a propagator until germination. They will not germinate below 13°C and do best around 20°C. Then the seedlings can be moved into a light, warm, well-ventilated position. The plants grow very quickly. When roots fill the pots, and weather conditions permit, they can be hardened off and then planted outdoors in a hole full of compost or even in the compost heap.

Courgettes are big plants with a wide leaf spread. They need plenty of water and should never dry out. It is better to water them in the evenings or early morning so that the moisture doesn't evaporate on warm days. A bottomless water bottle sunk into the ground next to the plant makes it easier for water to reach the roots. Courgettes should be cut when young; otherwise they quickly grow into marrows and the plant stops producing more courgettes.

SQUASHES

The Painting

Not only are the squash flowers beautiful, but the leaves are equally lovely. I painted the flowers of the squash, nasturtium and marigolds first and then washed Lemon Yellow over the main foreground leaves with a hint of Phthalo Blue, which merged into the yellow. This underpainting was left visible as the patterning on the leaves. The leaves in the background were less yellow and more blue was added. When all was dry, a richer, darker green was painted around the leaves and stems.

I find it is important to stand back from the painting to judge whether any details, such as a leaf or petals, need attention. The colour can be manipulated to give the effect of sunshine and shadow: increasing the colour intensity of the painting by adding more yellow in the foreground, more blue in the background and dark blue to the darkest dark is very effective.

The Gardener

Squashes are easy to grow but are temperature-sensitive. They need warmth to germinate. It is better to sow late and plant out when the weather is right for them and when the true leaves appear. They need plenty of water and rich soil and if they are planted in the compost heap they have both. When harvesting they should be cut with a section of stem attached to stop the fruit rotting. Drying them in the sun hardens the skin and helps with storage. The longer they are dried the longer they will store – probably for several months in a cool, dark, airy, dry place.

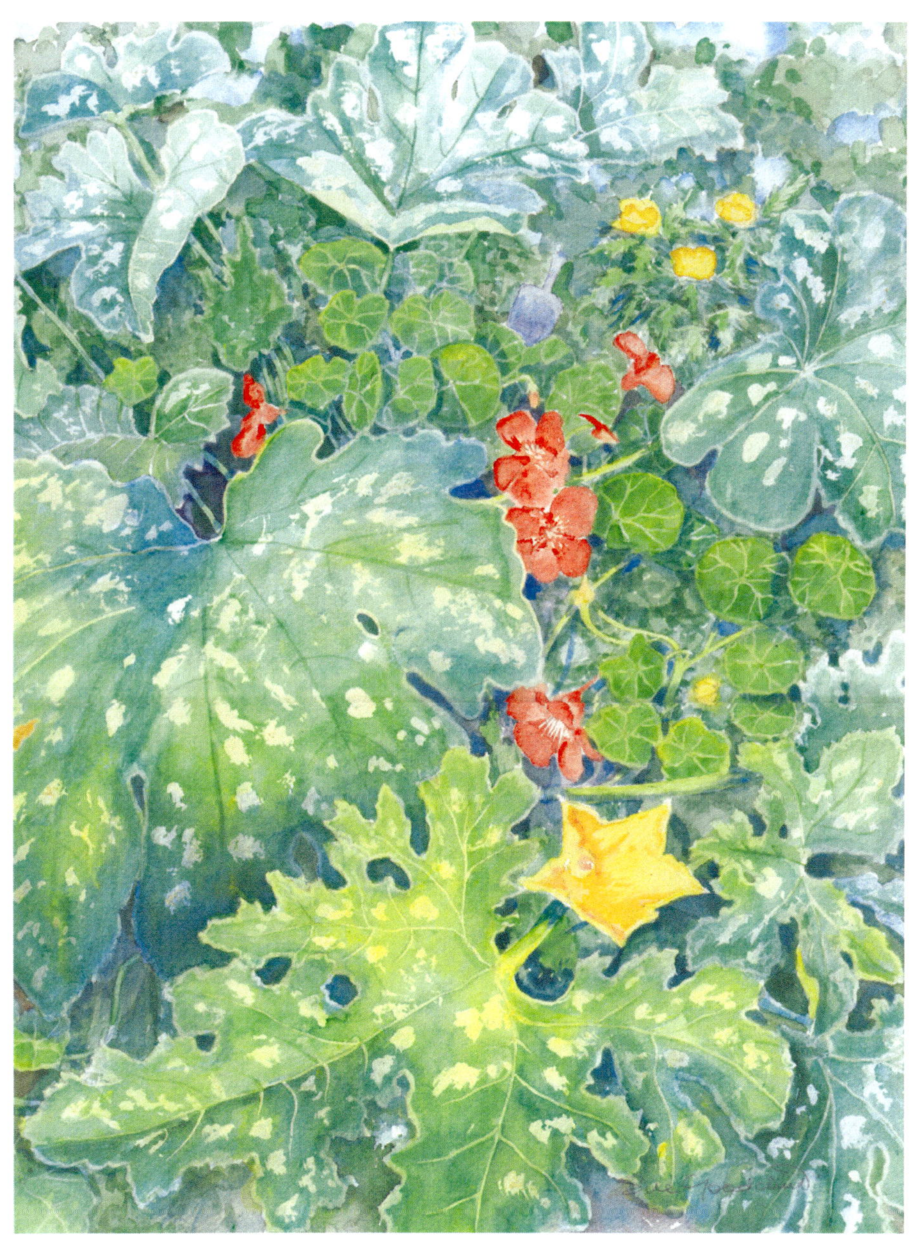

CUCUMBER

The Painting

This little sketch was painted simply with lots of greens and blues, but always with tonal values prominent. Tonal values play an important part in creating space and volume. In this subject, the light was from the left, which meant shadows on the right with shadows cast by one cucumber on to another. Cast shadows can cut across, giving a greater feeling of depth. Dashes of red used for the flowers were added to darken the green for the shadowed side of the fruit and stems.

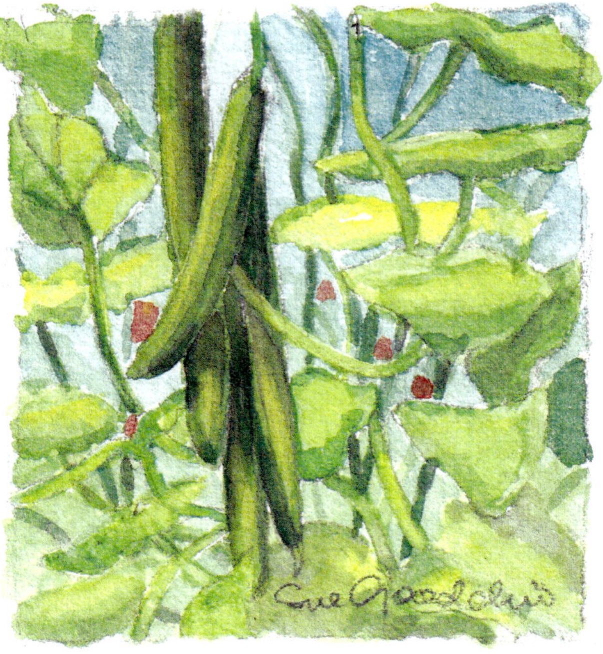

The Drawing

This is an ink drawing turned into mixed media by adding coloured pencil. I used various greens starting with the palest Grass Green over everything, but with very light pressure in high-lit areas. This was darkened with Emerald Green in the more shadier places, followed by Sap Green and Bottle Green on in the darkest, most shadowed sides and using more pressure. Finally Imperial Purple darkened areas such as the stem and leaf behind the cucumber, the tendrils and the prickles on the fruit, and a little was used on the shadow side of the fruit.

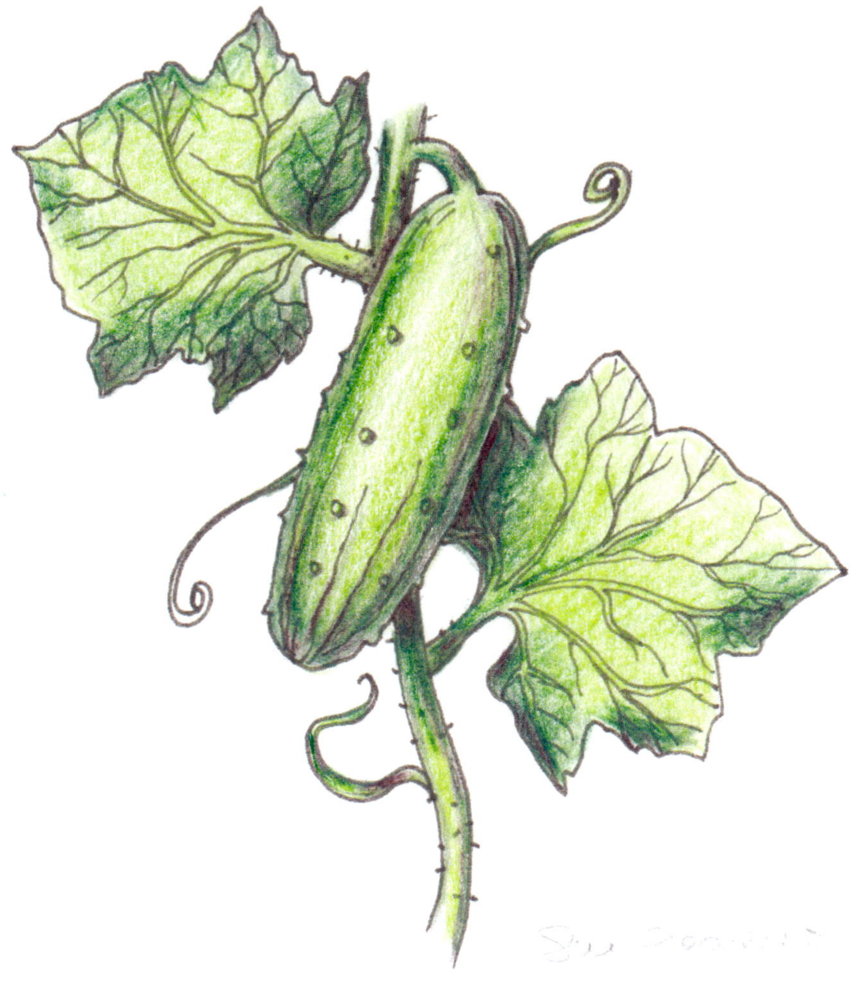

I made sure that the shaded parts accented the fruit with the lightest part in the centre. This gave a shape and definition. Tonal values are particularly important in defining contour and volume in terms of light and shade. The curve of the cucumber shows a gradual change from light to dark tones, and the area not in the light receives the darkest tonal value.

The Gardener
The cucumber is named *Cucumis*, a common name is 'cowcumber'. The cucumber is thought to have originated in North-West India, where it has been cultivated for more than 3,000 years, its wild ancestors being part of the human diet. Egyptians ate them at nearly every meal. In the Bible, the Israelites complained to Moses that they missed the cucumber they had enjoyed in Egypt. According to Pliny, the famous naturalist, philosopher and author of the celebrated *The Natural History*, Emperor Tiberius demanded fresh cucumber daily. They are now grown all over the world.

Seeds germinate quickly in warm soil – the warmer the soil, the faster the seeds sprout. Cucumbers do not like having their roots disturbed so do not transplant easily. It is best to sow into paper pots, which can be planted directly into the warm ground. The plants benefit from some shade from high temperatures to avoid bitter fruits. The seeds should be planted on their side with the pointed side downward – hence the water drains away, avoiding damping disease, to which cucumbers are prone. The old-fashioned ridge cucumber is the hardiest for outdoor growing and the most sweet and pleasant-tasting. Cucumbers grow fast and do not need a lot of care, except to train them and keep the soil moist. They are best staked because the fruits may distort if growing on the ground. A mulch of straw is important to keep the fruit clean and helps to deter slugs and beetles. The fruits can become misshapen or poor-tasting if moisture is inadequate or inconsistent. As cucumbers are heavy feeders they need plenty of organic compost prior to planting, and this helps retain moisture as well as nutrients. Cucumbers form their main roots close to the surface of the soil, so growing them in shallow containers gives a better yield than using deep pots. Research has shown that cucumber plants produce a pulse of salicylic acid – a medication used to help remove the outer layer of skin and used to treat warts, psoriasis, acne, ringworm and dandruff. It is a key ingredient in many skincare products. It was one of the original materials for making aspirin in 1897.

Cucumbers are best harvested when young so that the strength of the plant is not exhausted. The more cucumbers are harvested, the more they will produce. If allowed to become too big they become bitter. Lemon cucumber plants have smaller, rounded fruit. They should be harvested before turning yellow when they are full of seed.

FRENCH BEANS

The Painting

The best quality of paint is always important when using watercolour. Artist's-quality paints are more expensive, but they are more vibrant and give better results than student ranges. They contain more pure pigment and fewer fillers, additives or extenders.

I usually mix my own greens, but sometimes it is useful to have tubes of green. Hooker's Green is a dark, dull yellow green, giving natural foliage colour. It was originally devised for botanical illustration by the Victorian botanist Sir Joseph Dalton Hooker, director of Kew Gardens, London, and a president of the Royal Society. It was a mixture of Iron Blue and Genuine Gamboge. The modern mix is light-fast. Viridian is very light-fast, transparent, moderately staining, moderately dark, dull blue green. It was formerly the most common watercolour green used by masters such as J. S. Sargent. It gives a glowing, granulating green which works well when diluted. It needs patience to dissolve the pigment. Sap Green, however, can lose its yellow in sunlight.

In this painting I used both Hooker's Green and Viridian with the addition of Lemon Yellow in the foreground beans and leaf veins. The background green was darkened with the addition of a little Quinacridone Red used in the bean flowers.

The Gardener

French beans are half-hardy annuals which grow best in warm conditions. Early beans can be grown in the greenhouse or under cloches. Green-podded types are the most common. There are also yellow types. Sometimes French beans are known as string beans or kidney beans.

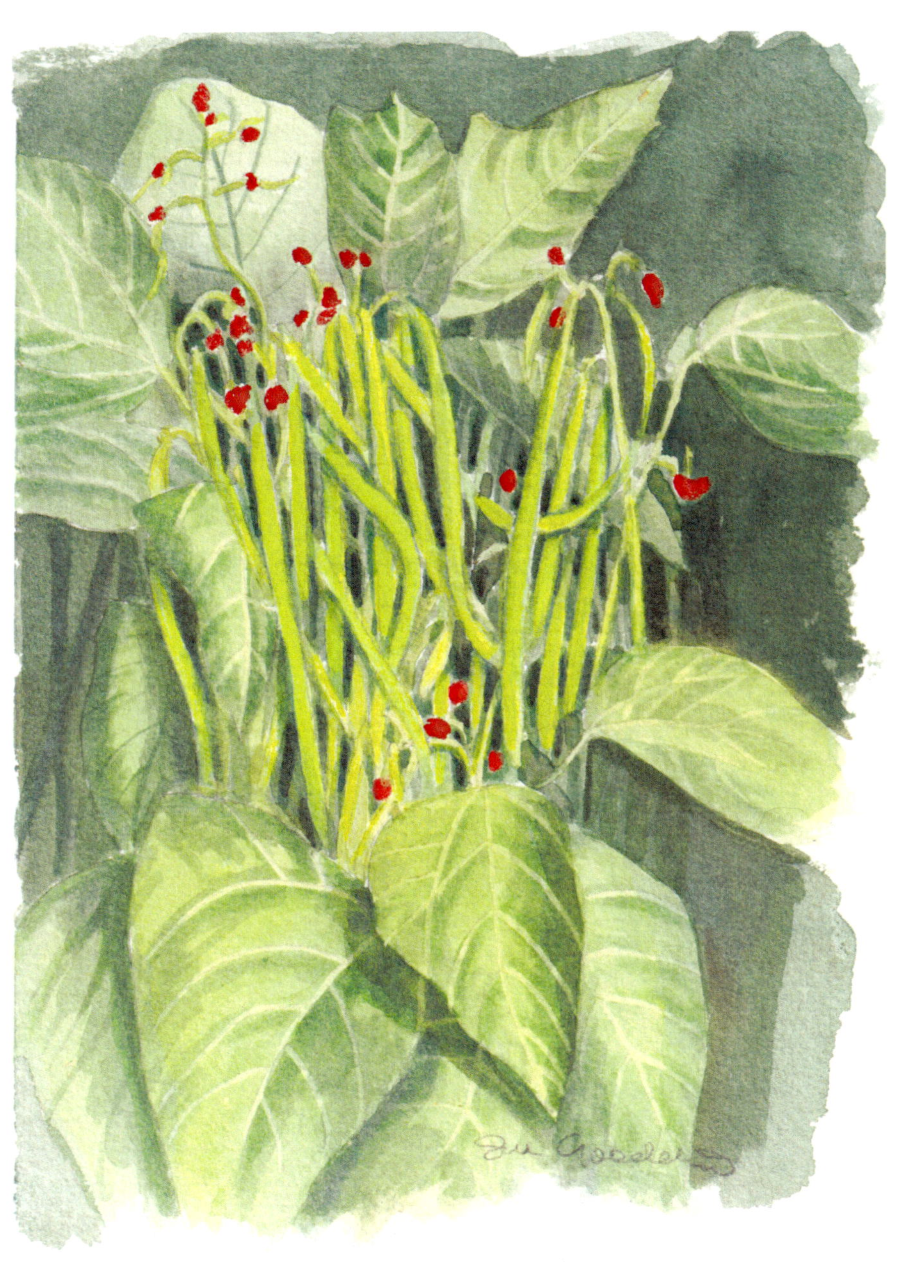

They are valued for their vitamin and mineral content.

Beans grow best in well-drained fertile soil with farmyard manure or compost dug in during the winter, though too rich a soil and too much fertiliser encourages soft growth and excessive leaf growth. Soil temperature should be at least 10°C to assure rapid germination. French beans do not thrive in cold soils and the seed can rot if too wet. Seeds can be protected under cover or with fleece or a cloche, but it is better to wait for warmer weather and use protection to guard against sudden temperature drops. Cloches or fleece retain warmth by creating a microclimate, raising the temperature of the soil before sowing. An open-ended cloche allows the plants to cool naturally rather than growing in heat which can produce mildew. A cool airflow protects the plants. Cloches also give winter protection, extending the growing season by retaining a little warmth and maintaining the quality of leaves and roots which could otherwise be weather-beaten. Interplanting beans among aromatic brassicas, garlic or mint, can confuse and deter unwanted insects.

Monthly sowings give beans throughout the summer. Later sowings may need cloche protection according to the weather. Harvesting regularly is essential to have young, tender beans. They should snap off the plant cleanly. Over-mature pods become stringy and show the beans bulging out of the pod walls. This is a flageolet bean, and when mature and dried it is a haricot bean.

CLIMBING FRENCH BEANS

The Drawing

Drawing is a slow, relaxing, but at the same time exciting process. One does not fully learn all the skills: learning

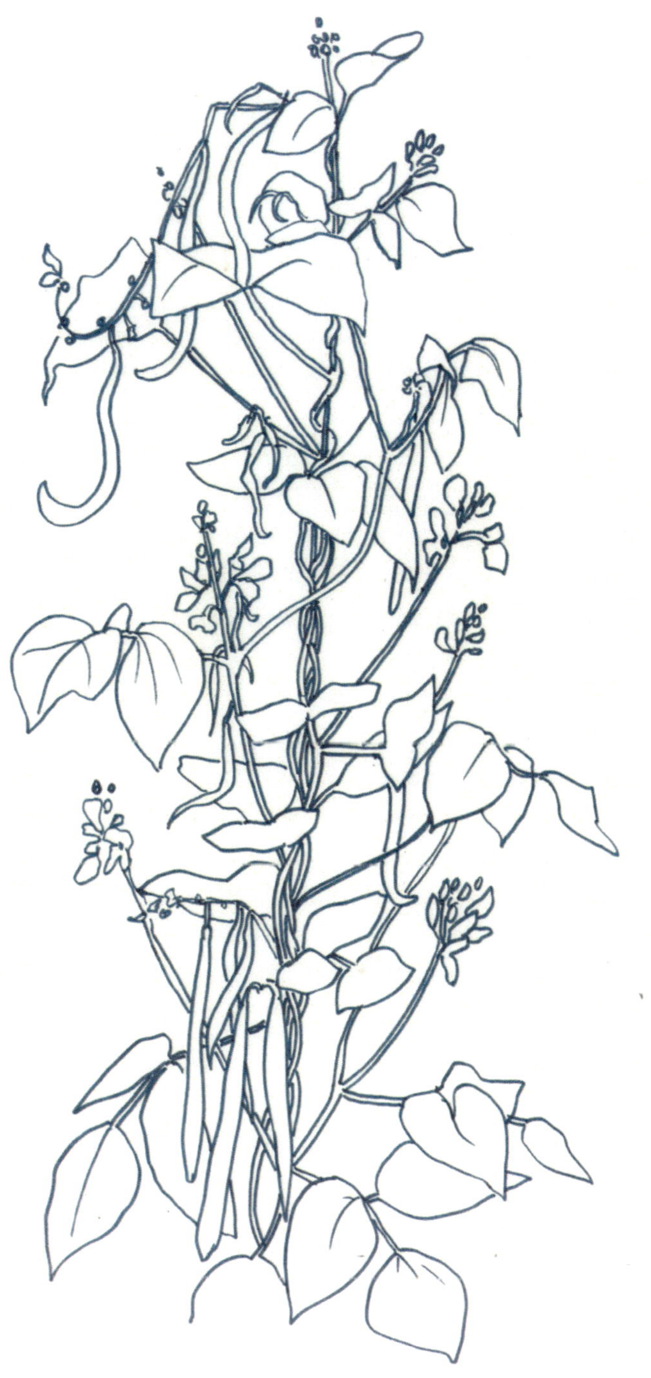

is a continuous process and each drawing provides a new perspective and enhances one's knowledge and skill. A drawing which concentrates on line will reflect the inner feelings of the artist and the achievement in its success. Versatile artists do not limit themselves to certain themes and subjects, but attempt to draw almost anything. It is important to recognise the spaces between shapes, noting where one line crosses another.

RUNNER BEANS

The Painting – Runner Beans and Melon

The first thing to establish is the message, with the focal point of the painting being the main story. This painting is about the beans and melon, but the eye goes straight to the pot, then back around to the vegetables. The background is played down so that attention is focused on the foreground, played down simply to support the focal point with a strong contrast of tones. This makes the background appear more subdued; otherwise there would be a conflict of interest. These elements need to be considered from the start so that the effect of light is not lost with successive washes.

The painting began with the background, building up texture and colour with successive layers of paint. The way the light and shade falls on the pot describes its volume and solidity, assisted by bright Lemon Yellow, then Indian Yellow merging into Permanent Violet. These colours need to be studied. Tone is the general term referring to qualities of lightness and darkness. Yellow is seen as a light colour and purple as a dark colour; this is exactly how I have used them on the pot, with yellow in

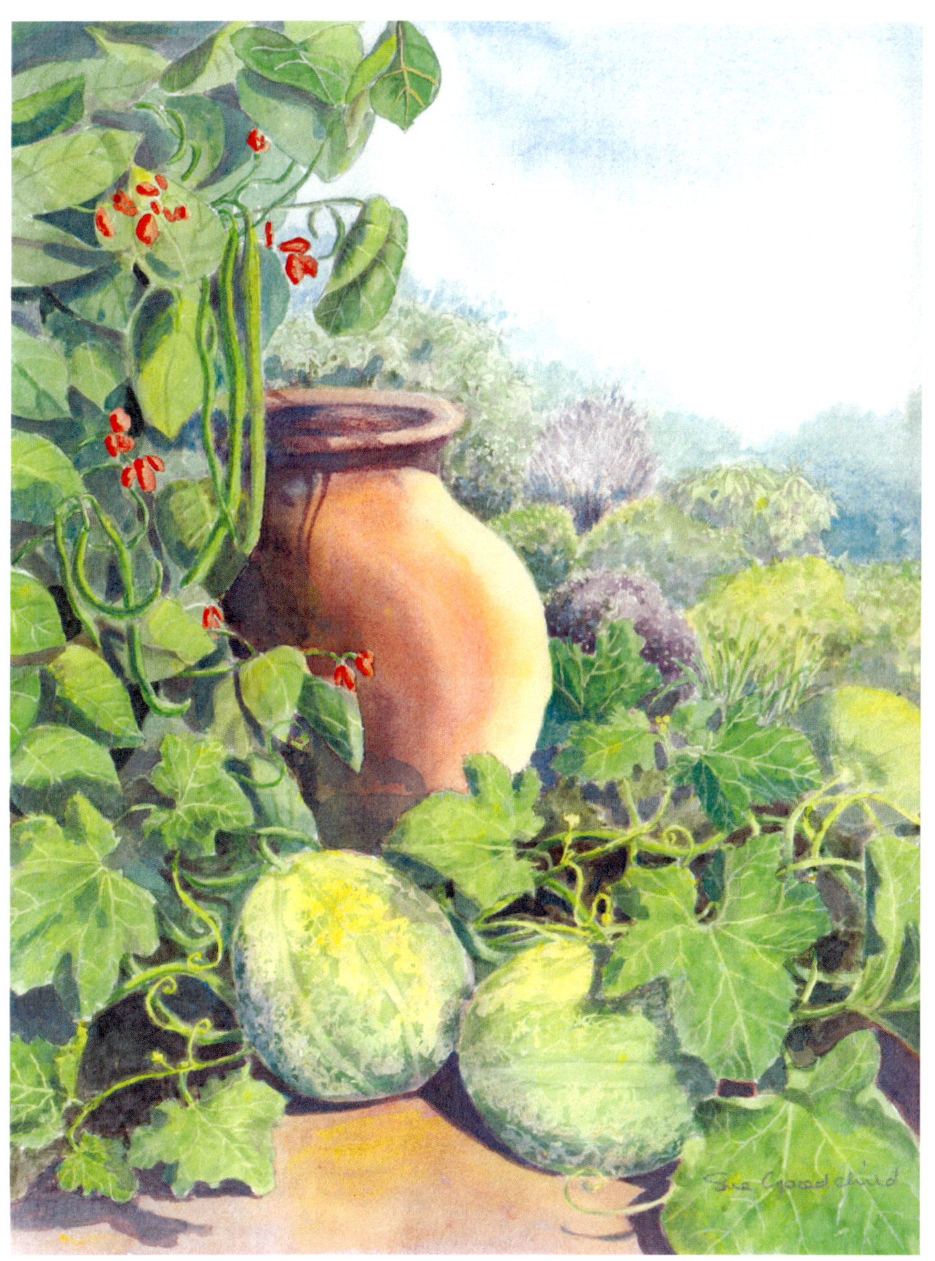

the leaves and purple in the shadows behind the leaves, fruit and beans, the transparent darks accentuating the intensity of the light.

The green was a mix of Cobalt Blue and Aureolin for the lighter layers and a touch of Burnt Umber for the darker areas, adding more umber to darken. Further layers were added, leaving lighter strips of the previous washes to denote the stripes. Pure blue was scumbled over the shadow side to denote reflected light.

Most objects show some reflected light, meaning the light and colour that bounce off other objects nearby. It can be an illuminating factor in shadows and is invaluable in helping to create a sense of volume. This effect is more easily seen in strong light. Reflected light is never as strong in the shadow areas as it is where the light hits an object directly. When looking at an object or shadow that contains reflected light, it helps to half close the eyes to be able to see tonal changes and to understand the distribution of light. Reflected light brings colour with it, and this increases perception and adds subtlety to the painting.

Violet was washed into various shadow areas on the pot, the ground and in between the leaves. In cool shadows there is often a warm glow of colour which enriches the depth of the shadow. I added a very light wash of Lemon Yellow to the leaves. The effect of light in watercolour can alter the perception of the subject, with the light transforming the ordinary into something extraordinary.

The Gardener

In the seventeenth century, runner beans were introduced from America purely as ornamental plants, grown for their lovely flowers. They are perennials that produce small root tubers, but are usually grown as half-hardy annuals.

To propagate runner beans, the seed should be sown in deep pots in a cool greenhouse and hardened off in a cold frame before planting out into warm soil, or they can be sown directly outdoors in late spring. Once they have germinated, the seedlings need as much daylight as possible. They are hungry and thirsty plants, so soil preparation is rewarded with excellent growth and yields. It was tradition for a trench to be dug in winter and filled with manure and compost. Another idea is to line the trench with newspaper and thoroughly soak it before adding the compost. During the winter this breaks down to a useable tilth, into which the plants were planted.

They prefer a sunny, sheltered site and need support. I use bamboo canes, cut from the garden, and support strings. Runner beans grow, fast so once they have twined around the poles they will soon begin to climb. When they reach the top of the poles, the growing point should be pinched out so that the plants bush out. They grow quickly, so need to be harvested every few days while young and tender, otherwise they become stringy. They are rich in vitamins A, B and C, folic acid and fibre. They freeze well.

RADISHES

The Painting

The radishes were painted quite loosely with small washes for each radish, lifting off colour in the centres to suggest light, which was done while the paint was wet using a dry brush. Each radish was darkened with richer colour, especially where one radish was against another and to accent the unpainted root. The shadow around the radish was painting with Permanent Violet, which was taken up and around the leaves, painted with light and dark green mixed from Lemon Yellow and Phthalo Blue.

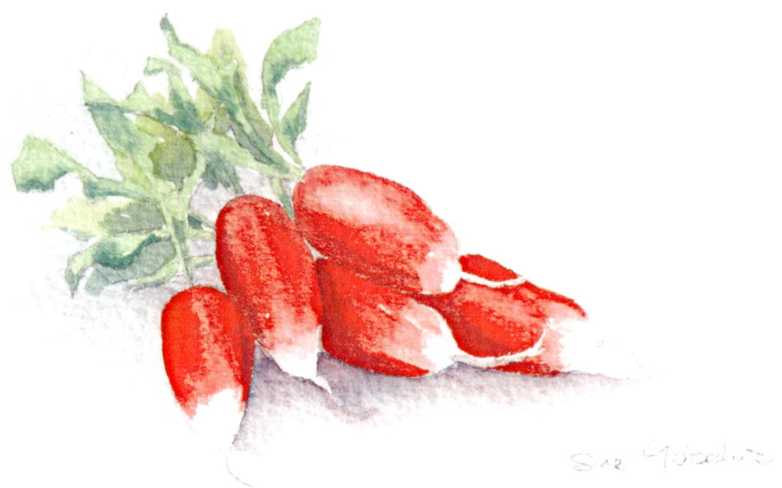

The Gardener

The seed should be sown directly into fertile, moisture-retentive compost. Radishes germinate within days, with the roots swelling quickly. They need a constant supply of water, otherwise they become woody, especially if they get too large, so they should be pulled regularly with sowings every few weeks giving a steady supply. Vegetables that mature quickly and are ready to harvest soon after sowing, such as radishes, need staggered sowing every two or three weeks to give a constant supply – in the case of radishes, every week. If allowed to form seeds, the pods are delicious. Pick pods when green and eat raw for a crunchy radish addition to salads. It is useful to add radish seeds to parsnip seeds when sowing. The radishes grow quickly before the parsnips, and they can be harvested before the parsnips germinate.

The roots are rich in antioxidants and have high levels of vitamin C and folic acid.

CELERY

The Painting
Drawing with a pencil is an excellent way of creating a three-dimensional image on a two-dimensional surface. I first drew with the soluble watercolour pencils and then wet the drawing with clear water. More colour was added while the paper was wet. I used varying greens and light violet. This mix of colours merged when wetted and formed a neutral colour.

The Gardener
Celery is a half-hardy plant that needs a sunny open position, a rich soil and plenty of water. A lack of water sends a crop to seed. I germinate them in a heated propagator, pot on the seedlings and grow them on in a cold frame before planting in the ground. The wider the planting, the bigger the plants. It is a hungry plant and responds well to preparatory work in adding compost, which helps the ground to hold water. Blanching by plunging the seedlings into a trench, or using cardboard collars around the stems, makes the stems succulent and sweet by reducing any bitterness. Self-blanching celery can be planted fairly close together and needs neither earthing up nor blanching collars to produce fine, tender stems. It has a good nutty flavour and grows easily.

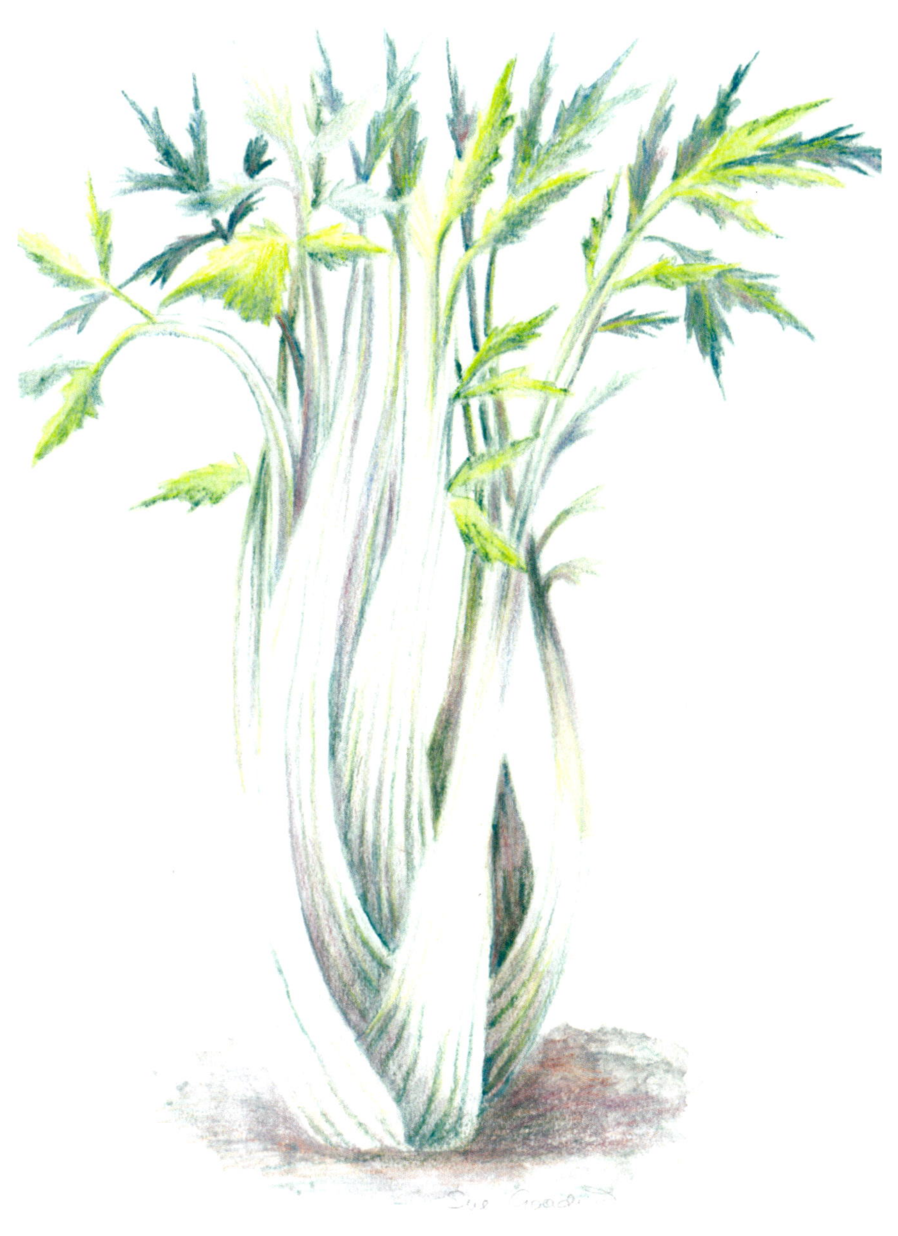

CELERIAC

The Painting

Sometimes the patterns created by dappled light can explain a subject without painting the plant itself. Creating a realistic picture means creating an illusion of space that can be communicated through various elements, such as line, to show edges sharp in the foreground and soft in the background. This contrast of value in the front and less in the background can give a sense of depth.

Dripping and spattering of paint can be achieved with either a toothbrush or a bristle brush. The paint is dispatched by bending the hairs of the brush with a finger and then releasing them in the direction of the paper. Dripping is a technique in which the pigment is brought directly to the paper surface by means of an overloaded brush. Spattering has a loose, free appearance and helps in unifying the painting. The speckled appearance can act as a gentle transition between two areas of different colours. A brush-load of paint tapped against fingers spatters colour across the damp surface. For more control, the brush is held close to the surface of the painting.

The shadows had a purple tone with some effects produced by local colour, surface texture and direct light. Basically only a few colours were used – Sap Green, Ultramarine Violet, Yellow Ochre and Burnt Sienna – with all colours mixed together for the darks.

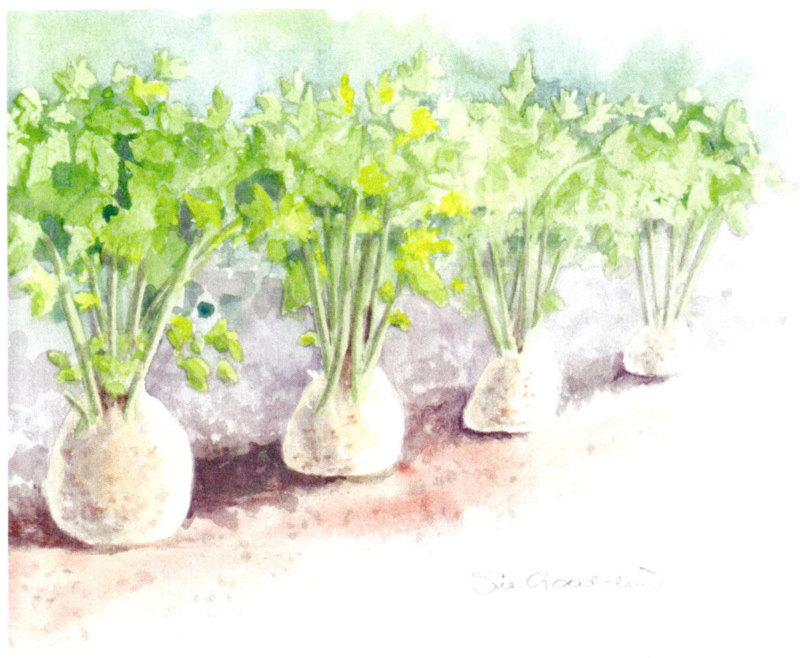

The Gardener

Celeriac does not need blanching as it is the root that is eaten. It is raised from seed in mid spring and planted out in early summer, taking about five months to harvest. It is a useful winter vegetable, making good soup, and can be roasted and puréed. It is very nutritious. Celeriac needs a long growing season in very rich soil and lots of water. I sow the seeds in early spring in the greenhouse, first in trays and then in pots, before placing the seedlings in a cold frame. They grow very slowly and may take weeks before they can be planted out. The soil should be drawn away from the plant and side leaves removed so that the swollen root stands out. They can be left in the ground all winter and used as required, though they are not completely frost-hardy and may need a protective mulch. They taste better if they remain in the ground until shortly before they are eaten. Slugs are the main enemy of the celery family.

CHICORY

The Painting

I couldn't ignore these beautiful bright-blue flowers, which decorate the edges of the lane – obviously escapees from a previously grown crop. The blue is so intense as to be breathtaking. I washed Cobalt Blue and Cerulean Blue in the lighter petals and Ultramarine Blue in the foreground petals, and a richer, thicker Ultramarine in the centre of the flowers. The sepals were also Ultramarine, painted with the tip of a fine brush. The hint of green leaves was used as a foil against the blue.

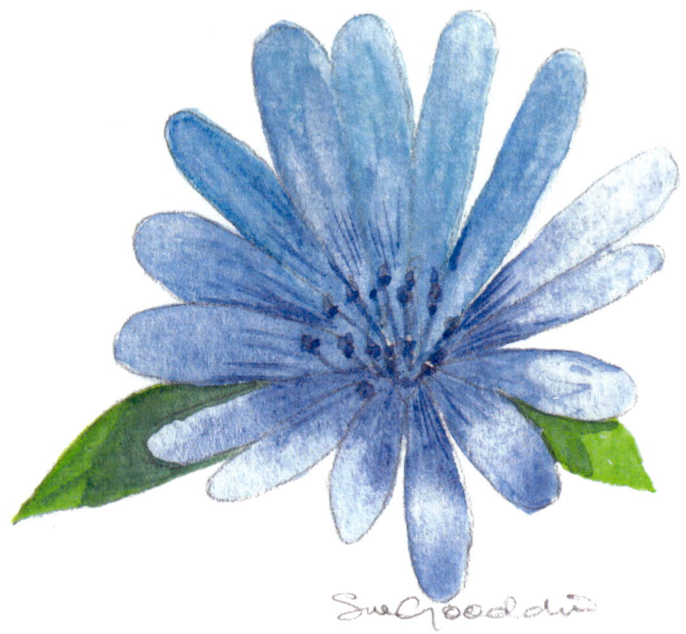

The Gardener

Chicory has long been an important plant, for both medicinal and culinary uses. Medicinally it is used for purging, to treat sore eyes, as a remedy for gallstones and as a digestive.

Seed should be sown in May and June, with non-forcing varieties in June and July, in an open sunny place. For mini leaves, sow indoors at any time. Individual leaves can be harvested as they grow, or harvest the entire plant two months after planting. The root can be left in the ground to grow new shoots in the following season. If left to flower, the plant produces the most beautiful blue flowers. There is a legend that the blue flowers are the eyes of a girl crying for her sweetheart lost at sea. Once the plant flowers the leaves become very bitter and must be boiled. The roots can be washed, chopped, roasted and made into chicory coffee.

A variety of chicory, *Cichorium endivia*, is sold as endive.

RADICCHIO

The Painting

A very attractive, inspiring vegetable – and I love the colour! I started with Quinacridone Magenta watercolour, leaving streaks of unpainted paper to represent the white veins. Keeping some dry areas into which the paint will not run, gives a hard edge. Laying a second application of paint while the first is still very wet allows the pigments to merge, giving a diffused effect with no hard edges. Once the paint was dry, I used pastel pencils to deepen the colour, taking note of light and dark areas, toning down the bases of the leaves and concentrating on making the painting work with light against dark and dark against light.

Combining transparent watercolour with opaque pastel can be exciting – building up layers, but allowing some underpainting to glow through. This creates depth and an intensity of colour.

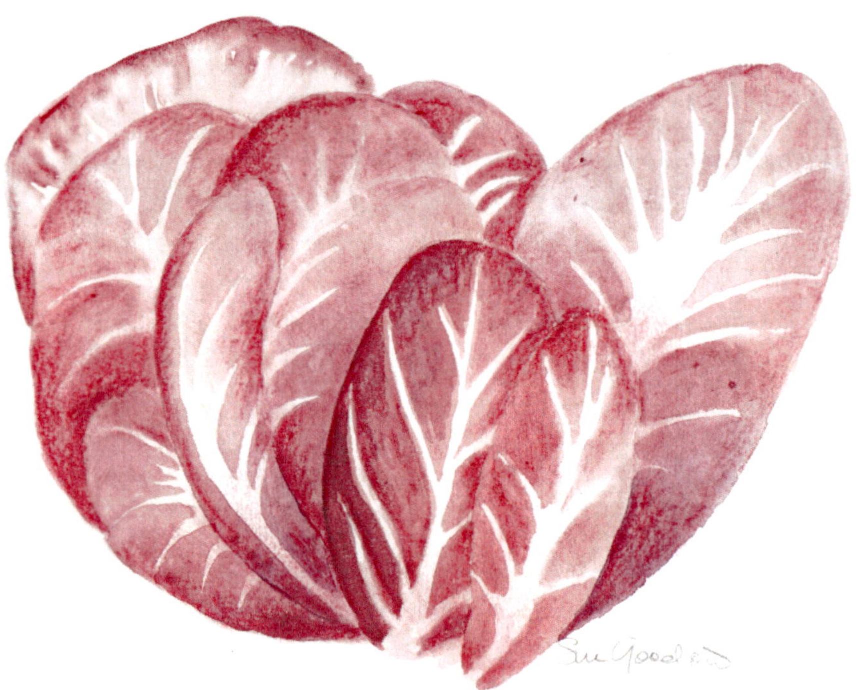

The Gardener
Radicchio is a perennial cultivated form of leafy chicory. It has a bitter and spicy taste which mellows if it is grilled or roasted. It belongs to the *Asteraceae* family, related to dandelions. It has dark reddish-purple leaves with white veins, looking similar to red or purple cabbage. It is a rich source of vitamin K, and also of Vitamins C and B6, iron, copper, phosphorus and potassium. It has many health benefits.

AUBERGINES

The Painting

Watercolour is a transparent medium which uses the paper as its source of white. The paper should shine through the pigment, with small areas of white paper reserved for highlights. I left unpainted paper for the shine on the fruit; and when all was dry, I used a damp brush to soften the edges and merge the shines. When a wash is laid around a highlight, it could, as in this case, dry with a hard edge. If there are too many highlights, the whites could be over-emphatic.

For a change I used Mars Violet, which is one of the oldest colours made from natural resources. It was the most coveted in antiquity because of its complexity of manufacture, making it extremely expensive, and it became a symbol of power and nobility. I mixed this with Burnt Umber for the dark of the fruit. This juicy dark was applied with rapid strokes while the other washes were still wet, but it was controlled by restricting the amount of water. To achieve transparency in even the darkest areas, the minimum number of brushstrokes were applied.

The leaves were painted with a mix of a warm yellow green mixed from New Gamboge and Cobalt Blue. The original Gamboge was yellow made from tree sap. New Gamboge is a non-toxic warm yellow, less opaque than Cadmium Yellow Deep and warmer than Indian Yellow. A darker green was used in places such as shadowed areas and along stems and stalks. This was mixed from Hooker's Green, with some of the dark used in the fruit.

The Gardener

Aubergines are in the same family as tomatoes and potatoes

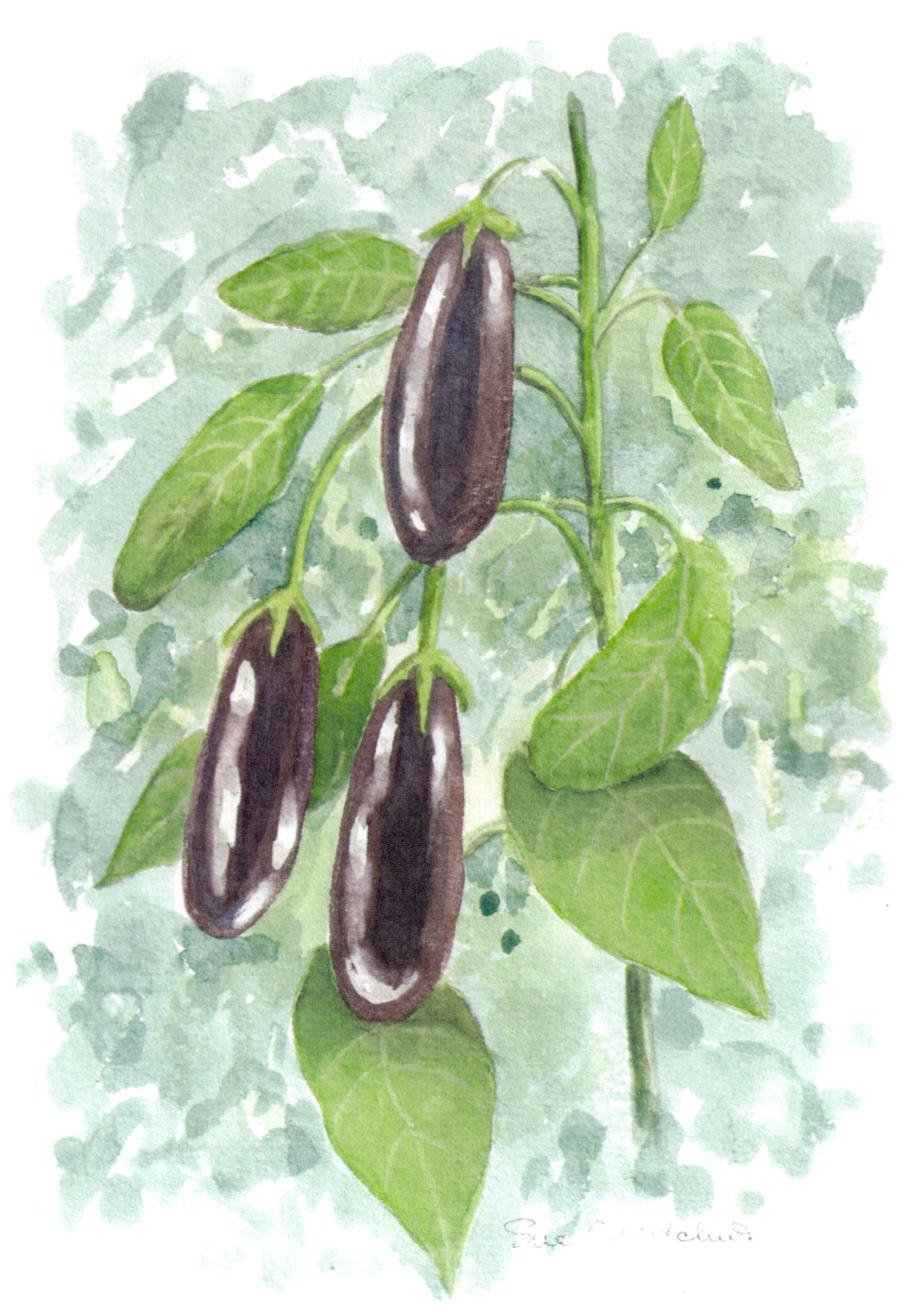

and, like tomatoes and peppers, need plenty of moisture. Sow from January to April in a warm greenhouse. Once the plants are growing well, pinch out the growing tip to encourage branching. Staking them upright ensures as much sun and air as possible gets to the fruits, which are coloured from deepest plum. If growing conditions are cool, the colour develops less. It is best to pick them as soon as they are large enough as they become bitter if left too long.

They supply heart-protective minerals found in the skin, such as potassium and beta-carotene. They are also a source of fibre and polyphenols, which reduce blood sugar.

PEPPERS

The Painting
Painting is a visual communication expressing thoughts and passion, hopefully capturing the artist's initial reaction to the mood, colours and tonal values of the subject. When observing colour, the trained eye differentiates not only rich colours but shades and tones. The untrained may be deceived into thinking a distant hill is the same green as something in the foreground because they know it is green – not because they are observing correctly. This applies to plants as well. A white flower may appear bluer in the cool morning light, but in the warmer afternoon can appear more yellow, deepening to orange as the sun sinks through the moisture-laden atmosphere. Colour is an important component of a painting. It can be changed by light, producing subtle harmonies and tones. Colour and light are intertwined, and their constant change is a

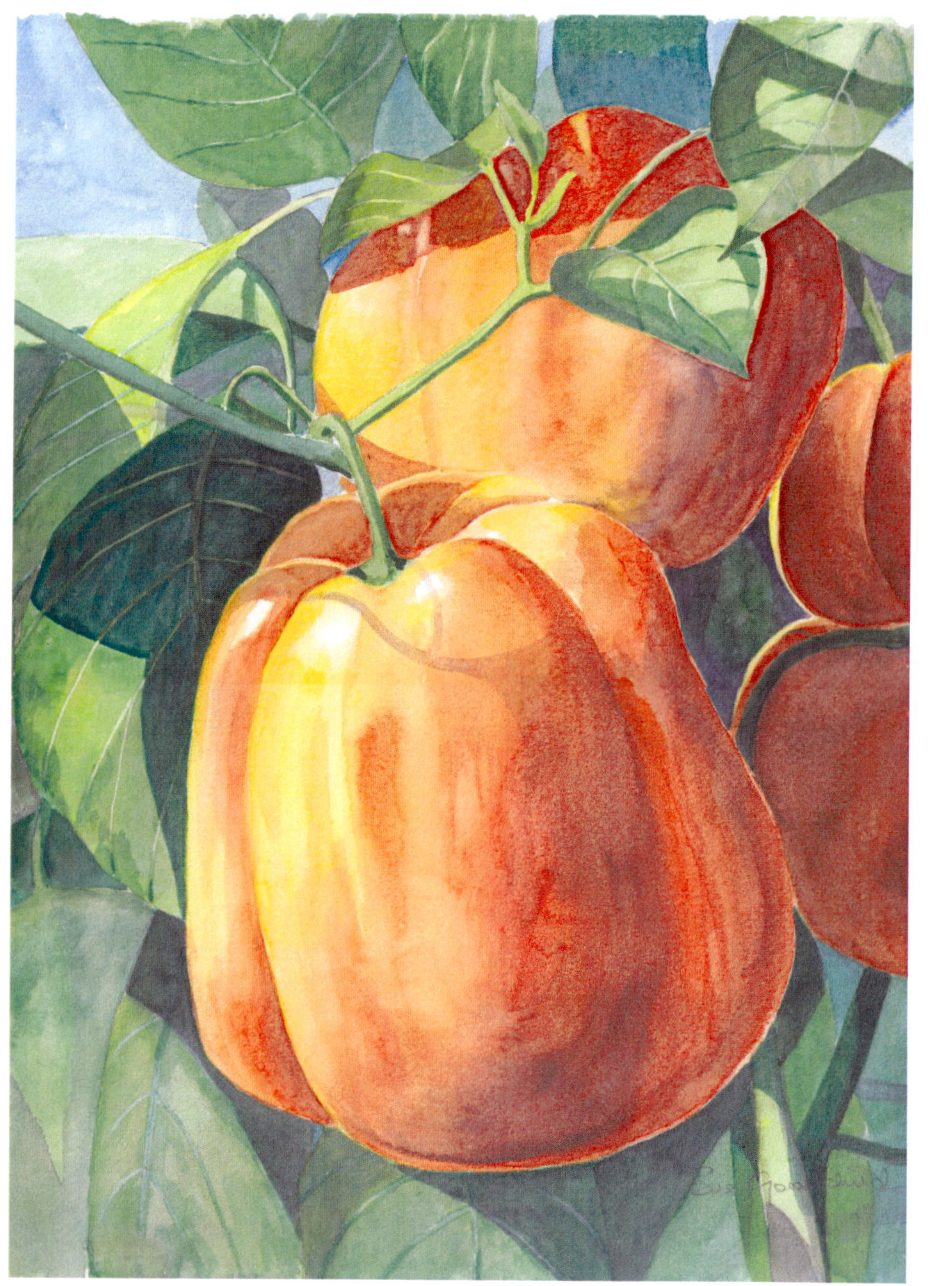

difficult challenge to capture in paint. Light affects colour in that it enables one colour to borrow from another, and watercolour is ideal for interpreting this beautiful effect. A hue can bleed into its neighbour, uniting the two in a delicate relationship. It is important to remember that every colour reacts to its neighbour, never working in isolation.

These peppers were given thin washes of strong yellow, quickly followed by orange highlights and sienna in the shadows, thinking only in terms of line and tone and letting colour and colour temperature provide the structure. These cool greens against the warm colours of the fruits can encourage interest in the focal area. When distinguishing the tone of a colour, its lightness or darkness, its hue is important. For example, Cadmium Red and Venetian Red are the same hue, but they are different in tone. Degas said, "Painting is the art of making Venetian Red look like Vermillion."

The Gardener

The seeds should be sown in a propagator in trays or pots of seed compost. Pots are more practical as the seedlings can be planted more easily. Both red and green fruits grow on the same plant –green when young, red as they age. They are best picked when young and green to encourage further cropping.

Plants grown outdoors in pots can be moved out in June and placed against a warm south-facing wall, which will protect them from cold winds. Each plant needs a support cane and regular watering with a liquid feed every fortnight from summer onwards. I find it better to use nutrients derived from plants, such as potassium from comfrey. Prepared feeds can cause overfeeding and result in an imbalance, leading to problems.

SPINACH

The Painting

Due to the crinkly nature of the leaves, I started with Sap Green, leaving unpainted paper for the highlights, and added Hooker's Green in between these and the veins. More darks were added to shaded areas, mixing Burnt Sienna into the Hooker's Green for the darkest places under the leaves.

During the work I stand back from the painting to see it from a distance. This filters out a lot of detail and helps to make a more objective assessment of values. It is most useful is looking at the painting several hours later or the next day when the mind is fresh and can observe the work critically. As it happened, I needed more darks.

The Gardener

Spinach is very rich in iron and has a high protein content. It is also rich in vitamin A. It is even more healthy if eaten raw, as cooking halts the absorption of calcium and iron. It is a cool-season crop and runs to seed in warmth and when daylight hours increase. It is best sown in spring or early autumn in situ as seedlings are difficult to transplant. It is best eaten young, cutting leaves at ground level as new leaves will grow. This also delays bolting. It needs lots of water and although it prefers full sun will last longer in the shade.

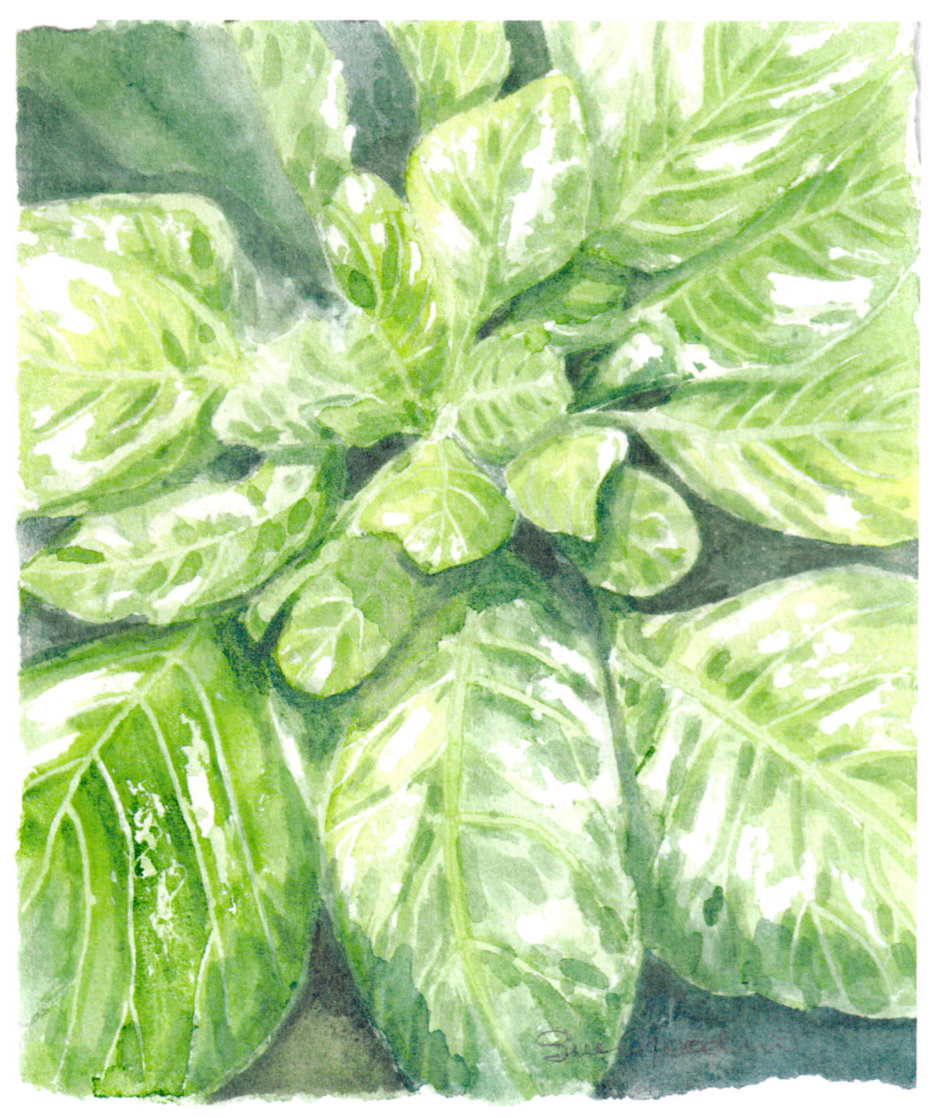

KALE

The Painting

A painting is a journey into the unknown. We begin with the artist's response to the subject, then the information available and lastly the demands of the painting, which culminate in the resulting picture. This painting was great fun as I used my favourite colour – purple. This was placed against the yellow green on purpose to create maximum impact. The tonal contrast of the light on the upper and outer leaves of the plant against the darker interior played a large part in the drama. To make the colour seem brighter I thought carefully about the surrounding colour rather than the colour itself.

I kept in mind that texture can be forgotten in shaded areas, so the texture ran from the light into the shade, knitting the two areas together. A sense of light, form, space and movement, as well as colour, tone and texture came about as a result of fine observation and love of nature.

The Gardener

Kales are easy to grow. They are exceptionally hardy, with even a harsh winter doing them no harm. They are not exacting in their soil requirements so long as there is good drainage and no waterlogging. Also, they are resistant to clubroot diseases, unlike other brassicas. There are two main groups: curly and plain-leaved. The curly kales are referred to as Scotch kales, and the plain are best known as cottager's kale and thousand-headed kale. If the centre of these is harvested while still young and small, they will produce tender young shoots, providing continual pickings of leaves. The large leaves are unpalatable. Flat-

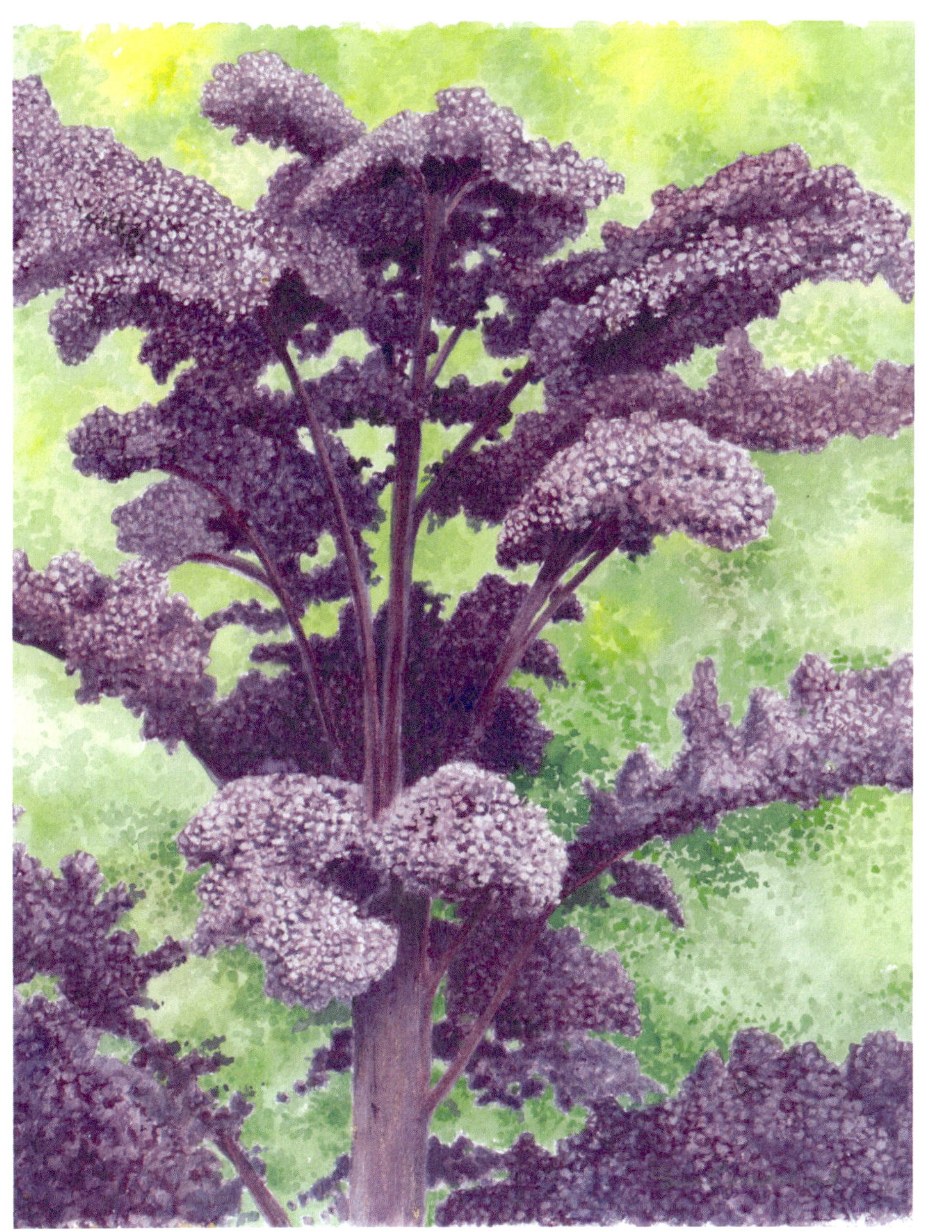

leaved kales, such as Red Russian, are among the sweetest and most tender. Black Kale is good for slow cooking. To prevent young plants becoming leggy, they can be grown in the shade. They need to be firmly planted and if interplanted with nasturtiums, insects can be distracted. There is a hybrid between the two called Pentland Brig, which is hardy and heavy-cropping. The navy-blue kale looks stunning when underplanted with marigolds.

CHARD

The Painting

I decided to expand the exciting scarlet of the chard into the foreground flowers and have a hint of it in the background. The green appeared even brighter surrounded by these stunning colours. Even the most brightly coloured painting can look flat if it lacks tonal contrast. The light on the leaves is accentuated by the tonal value and also the intensity of the colours.

I chose differing angles of the leaves as this helps to lead the eye around and back to the main image. The cast shadow underneath the chard leaves is the darkest area, and here the flower colours are accentuated giving an even deeper feeling of shade. The combination of cool and warm shadows creates a richer more luminous look. Flowers are at their best in their natural surroundings, and painting them outdoors is both rewarding and enjoyable. The flowers were observed from different angles and positions, some close up and then arranged to create the painting foreground. The background was painted using the colours already used in the painting along with Permanent Mauve accenting the brightness of the chard leaves.

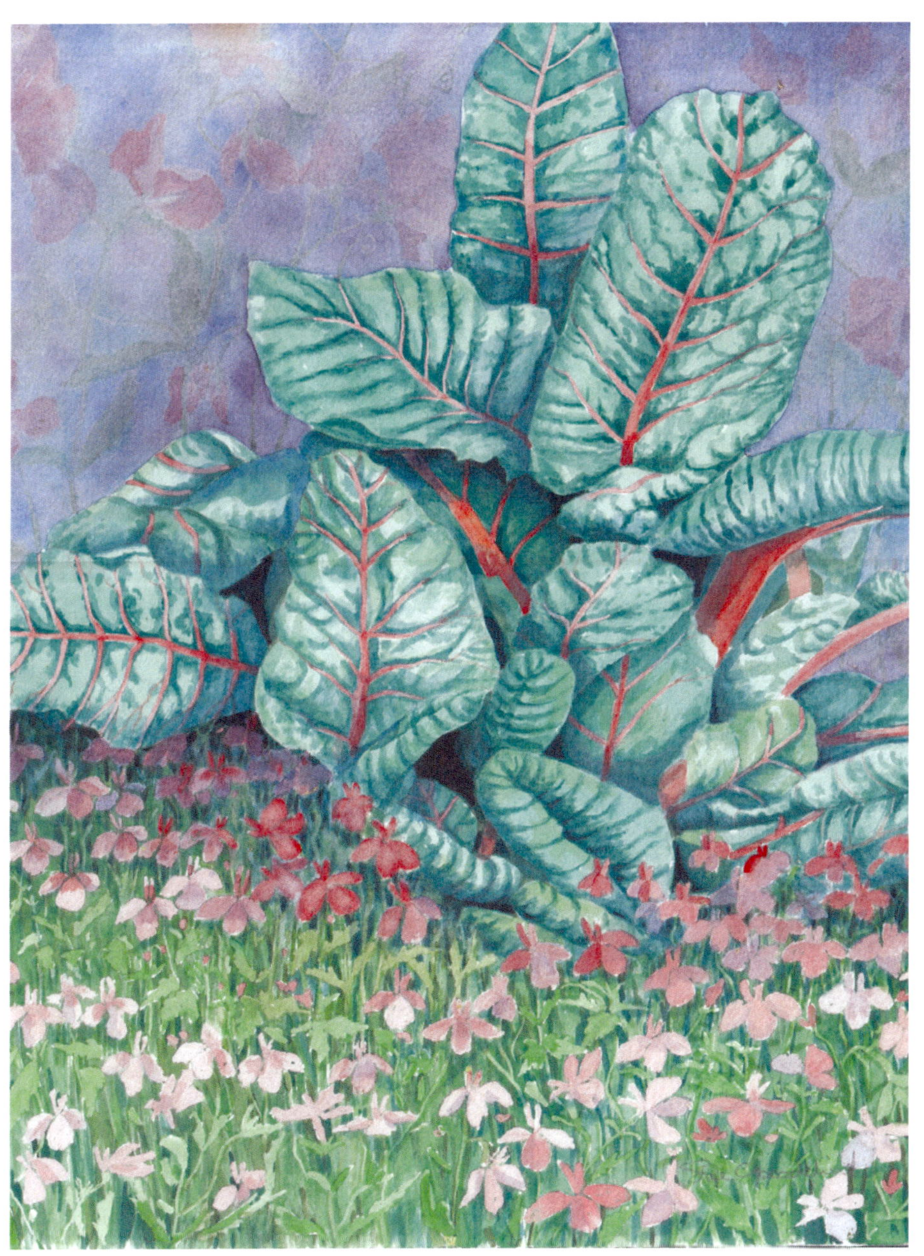

The Gardener
Swiss chard is a close relative of beetroot and spinach. Swiss chard, ruby chard and rainbow chard all taste very similar once cooked. Rhubarb chard is similar but has bright-crimson stalks and leaf veins. It is an ornamental adornment to any mixed border, enhancing the colours of the surrounding flowers. When harvesting, I usually take a few leaves from each plant so that new, fresh ones can grow on. The stalks can be chopped into pieces and used like seakale, which is grown for its tender shoots.

Sow in mid to late spring in a really rich moisture-retentive soil. Apart from thinning the seedlings, they need no further attention except for hoeing and watering in dry weather. An autumn sowing will give leaves in spring. I let the older plants seed and the resulting seedlings can be transplanted elsewhere. Being very hardy, they push up new leaves in spring even after a hard frost. Older leaves can be taken to the compost heap, allowing the light to reach new, fresh leaves. The advantage of an early autumn sowing is that they can follow on from previous vegetables.

CABBAGES

The Painting
The cabbage outline was drawn in pencil with the veins and raindrops masked so as to retain the white of the paper before flooding in various greens throughout the whole painting. The older, foreground leaves were washed over with a warm green mixed from Ultramarine Blue and some Lemon Yellow; the middle leaves were painted using Phthalo blue and a little Lemon Yellow in

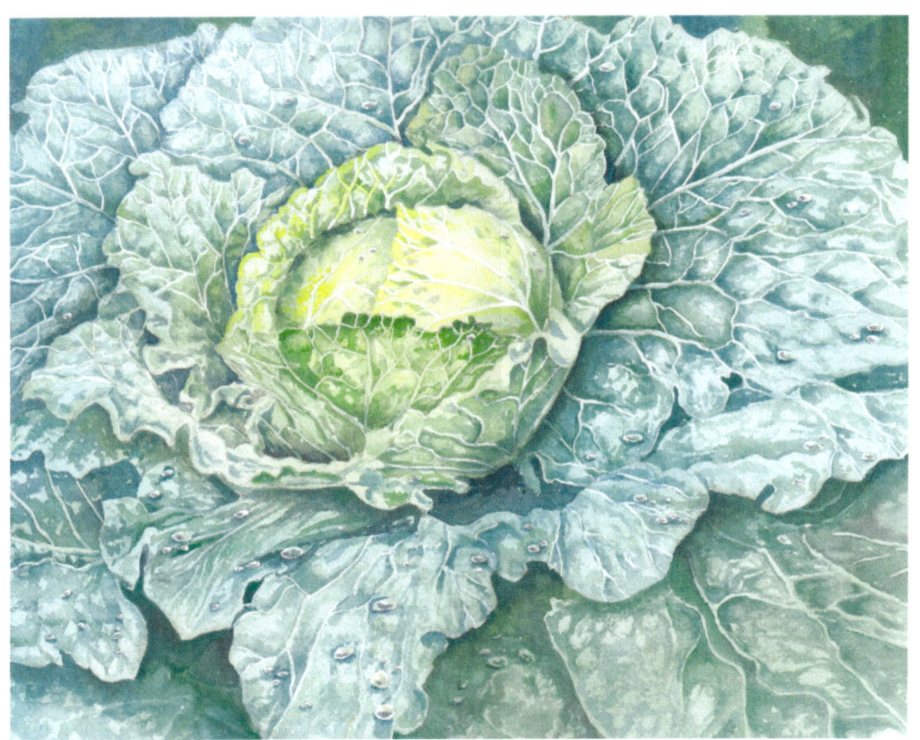

the mix; and the heart of the cabbage was painted with a green containing more yellow. When the paint was dry, the mask was removed, and the veins were toned down using various greens, with the veins in the heart a yellow green. Shadows around the edges of the leaves were a darker green painted over the inner veins, with the veins in the heart painted over with a dilute yellow. The raindrops were shaded using the dark green, leaving white paper where they caught the light. The background was a mix of greens with more blue in the mix to give a textured appearance.

Watercolour is an ideal medium for capturing the subtleties of different light effects. Unlike oil painting, which can be corrected and manipulated, watercolour loses freshness and transparency if treated in the same

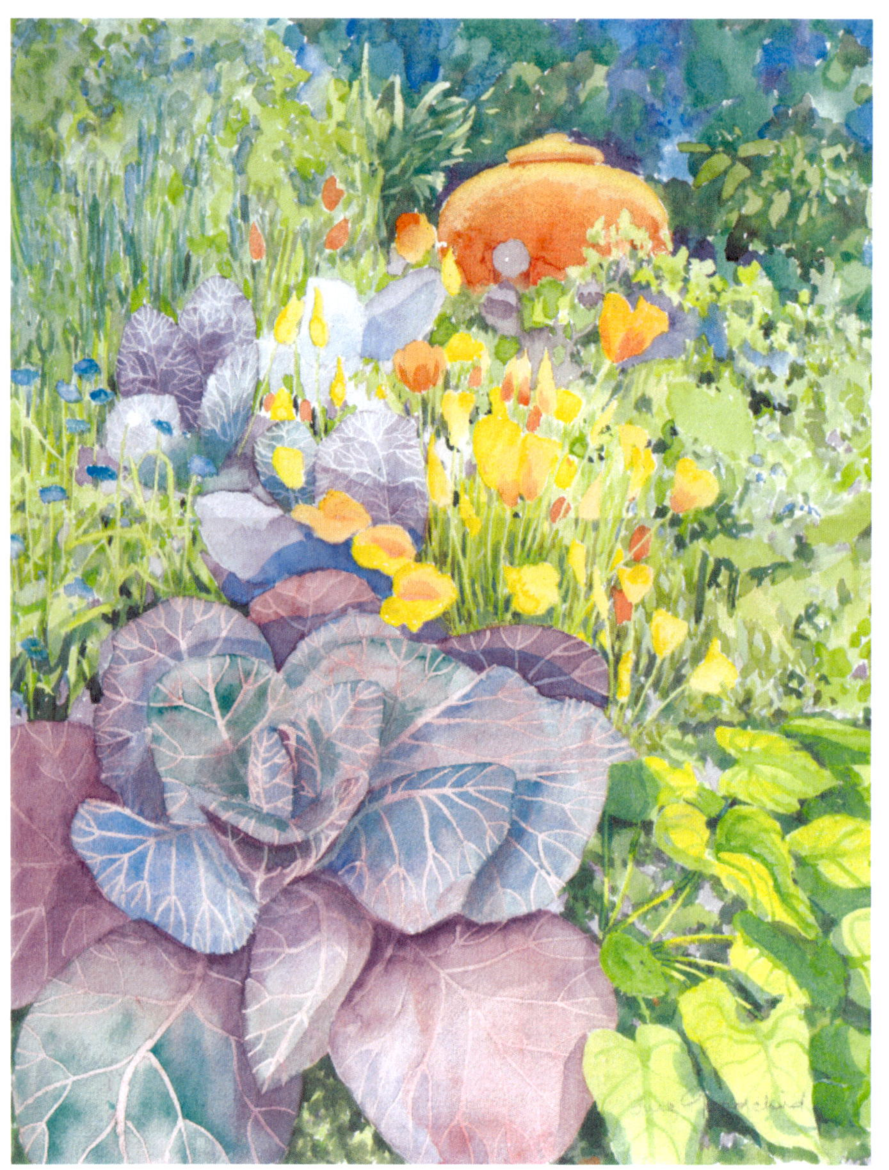

way. The exciting bright light and the contrasting of warm against cool colours – orange against purple – is dramatic. The more dramatic the difference, the more vibrant the painting. Cool blues in the background also complement the yellows in the foreground and accentuate the yellows of the pot. Surrounding colours can change the perception of that colour.

When applying pure yellow I make sure the palette is absolutely clean as even the smallest trace of another colour will dull or dirty the yellows.

Tonal values are also important in how we see the light and dark on an object relative to its surroundings. The more the contrast is developed within the tonal values, the more interesting and magical the painting. Colours can be beautifully rendered by placing small dabs of colour next to each other, as I have done in the background. When viewed from a distance, they appear to merge. I apply the most saturated pigments and darkest tones when the painting is nearing completion.

The Painting – Red Cabbage

Passion and inspiration are not simply a case of powerful feeling and blindly splashing paint around. To create atmospheric conditions one must have a clear vision of how the painting will evolve. This generates confidence to control the light source and the varying colours, and imbue the subject with imagination. It is important to gain as much information as possible from the subject before starting to paint.

A wet watercolour wash of Ultramarine Violet, Viridian and Rose Madder was indiscriminately painted across the paper. A graded wash starts with the pigment and a little clean water added with each stroke lightens the

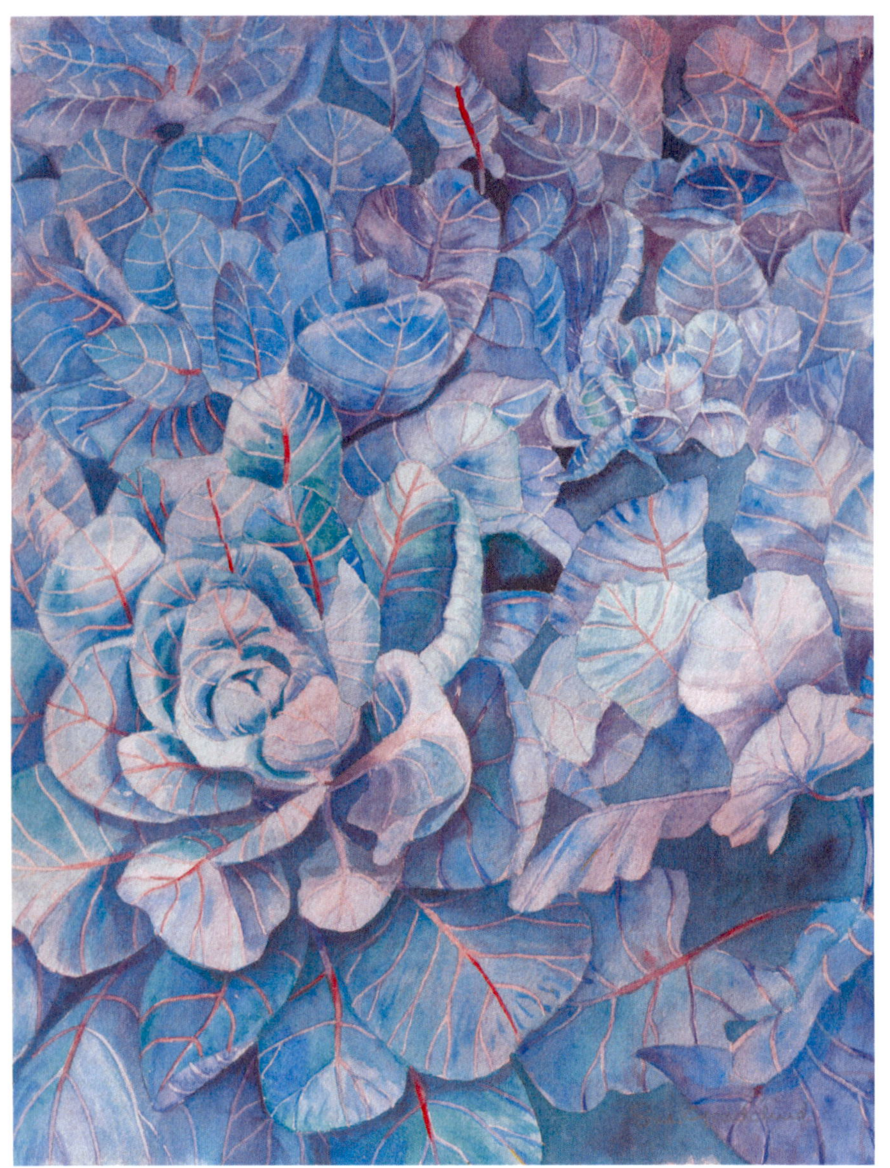

mix. The ratio of water to pigment is critical. Watercolour is a transparent medium, and by laying a second wash over a dried colour a third colour is produced where the first shows through. It is essential that the first colour is completely dry before adding the second; otherwise the first will be disturbed, creating a patchy look with no transparency.

This established a basis on to which shapes and tones were built. Some areas formed a shallow pool of colour with hard edges; and where I wanted these to soften, a dampened paintbrush removed excess paint. Fine lines and hard, dark edges were made with a kolinsky sable brush. The tapering fine point gives maximum control and makes it possible to draw with accuracy.

The Gardener

Cabbages do well by following a crop of legumes, which will have left nitrogen in the soil via their nodules. Seeds should be sown in spring in seed trays, and the seedlings should be pricked out into individual pots when large enough, before planting out in the garden in late spring to harvest in autumn to early spring. Make sure that the roots are firmly anchored as the growing cabbage head will become heavy and the wind may be a problem.

We love red cabbage for its taste as well as its beauty. Red cabbage needs a long period of growth, so it can be sown in mid spring, but the best crops come from a sowing in late summer or early autumn. They are perfectly hardy and can be left in the ground until spring. The bright colours of their foliage are attractive in flower borders or pots. Large white and small white butterflies seem to avoid it, probably preferring the taste of green cabbages, which can be stripped bare.

Spring cabbage is often given too much room. Planted closer together they protect one another. A first sowing of the early variety can be made in February under a frame or cloche, with further sowings in mid and late spring and successional sowings in early summer. They produce more leaves in response to a steady water supply. A fine mesh covering protects the plants and a rough mulch helps to deter slugs.

PAK CHOI

Pak choi, also known as Chinese cabbage, bok choy, white mustard cabbage, Chinese celery cabbage, horse's ear, Chinese flowering cabbage, Peking cabbage or snow cabbage, is related to Western cabbage. It looks like flat celery, having white, chunky stalks and deep-green leaves. It is valued for its broad, crisp, spoon-shaped leaf stalks, tasting like mild cabbage and spinach, and is best used raw, in stir-fries or lightly steamed. It has a mild flavour with a hint of mustard. Purple-tinged cultivars, such as red choi, are attractive in salads. Whole heads can be harvested in autumn and produce tasty flower shoots in early spring. It is available all year.

MUSTARD GREENS

Mustard greens are members of the *Brassica* genus, grown for their peppery leaves, adding colour, texture and spice to winter dishes and eaten raw in salads. They have broad wavy-frilled leaves, having a crunchy texture. There are white, red and green varieties. The seeds can be sprouted and eaten raw or dried to make the condiment mustard. The mustard plant contains volatile oils which have strong antimicrobial properties and antioxidants, are anti-inflammatory with compounds that have cancer-preventing benefits.

Mustard is native to India – hence its name of Indian mustard, but it is also known as Chinese mustard and leaf mustard. It prefers rich organic nutrient dense soils in full sun and cool temperatures for fast growth. It is sometimes grown as green manure, covering the soil to suppress weeds between crops, then cut down and dug into the earth.

FLOWERS

Certain flowers, like marigolds perform a useful role when palnted among such vegetables as cabbages. They exude chemicals that repel pests and attract pollinators, and, as with nasturtiums, forget-me-nots and cornflowers, they add a splash of colour which lifts the spirits, as can be seen in this painting. It was painted quite loosely with the orange and yellow echoed in all the flowers and the blue mixed with the yellow for the green.

Chives help to repel aphids and deter carrot fly, as do chrysanthemums, adding another colour burst of purple and orange. I also plant garlic around the edges of susceptible plants. Slugs and snails are a different matter – I try to encourage hedgehogs and birds and live peacefully with nature.

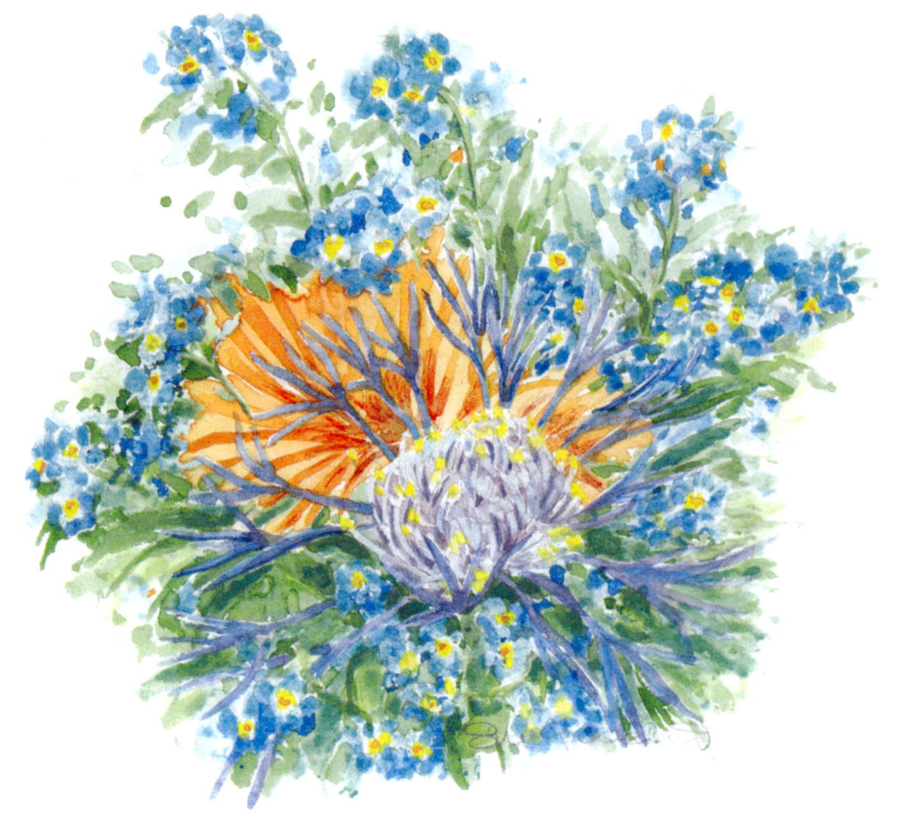

TURNIP

The Painting

The turnips were painted first using Quinacridone Violet, leaving unpainted paper around the bases of the vegetables. The leaves were painted with Sap Green, leaving streaks of white to represent the leaf veins. Some darks were added to the background leaves and then more Burnt Umber was added to the green to create a dark for the background, which was started with a light tone at the top; and as I worked down, I loaded the brush with more and more pigment. The darkest area contained almost no water and lots of pigment. Some Burnt Sienna was added in the foreground and then a shadow around the turnips was added using violet, which darkened because of the underpainting.

The white surface of the paper reflects back through the watercolours, giving them a wonderful luminosity.

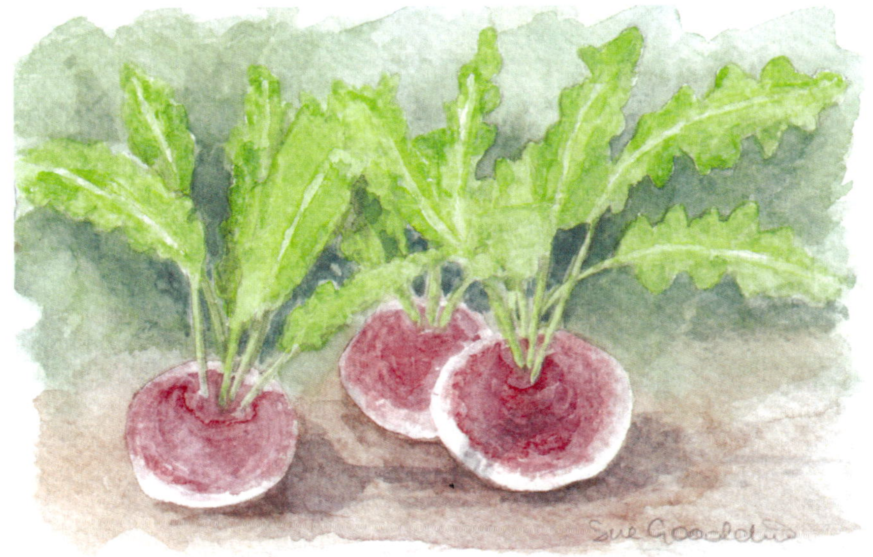

The Gardener

Pliny the Elder considered the turnip one of the most important vegetables of his day, providing fodder for animals as well as humans. Turnips were a staple crop before being replaced by the potato in the eighteenth century. The upper part of the turnip is white-skinned, protruding above the ground, and purple, red or green where the sun catches it. The interior flesh is completely white. The leaves can be eaten in a similar way to cabbage, being particularly high in vitamin A, B and C. They are milder after cooking. Baby turnips can be eaten raw in salads.

Turnips need cool weather to germinate and then grow quickly. High temperatures cause the roots to become woody. Thinning the seedlings is important for good-sized roots. Slugs love the seedlings, so the seed is best sown in pots before planting out. Turnips thrive in light, well-drained, firm soil, rich in humus, and the size and quality of the roots are improved when well-watered. In my dry garden I find it good practice to sow in the lee of a taller crop to give the turnips shade for at least part of the day.

The main crop is sown in summer for winter use, but earlier sowings can be made under cover in February, and late sowings in September of winter varieties provide spring greens, which are the edible new growth of young leaves. Turnips are biennial plants, storing nutrients in the root and flowering in their second year. They produce tall yellow flowers and pea-like pods, and then they die.

Turnips have health benefits, such as lowering blood pressure, fighting cancer, improving bone health, helping digestion and boosting the immune system. The root is high in vitamins C and K, calcium and lutein.

Swedes need similar conditions to turnips, but are slower

to mature. They are milder and hardier than turnips and can remain outdoors all winter to be lifted as required. Any left in the ground will grow edible tops. The lack of rain in the area where I live means they do not develop well, so I no longer grow them.

SWEETCORN

The Paintings

I drew the kernels in a spiral fashion, painted their lower parts with Yellow Ochre leaving dots of unpainted paper to represent shine and then darkened the base of each with Burnt Umber. The outer sheath was a mix of ochre tinged with some of the green used in the background. Likewise, the leaves around the cob were in Yellow Ochre and green and then darkened with Burnt Umber.

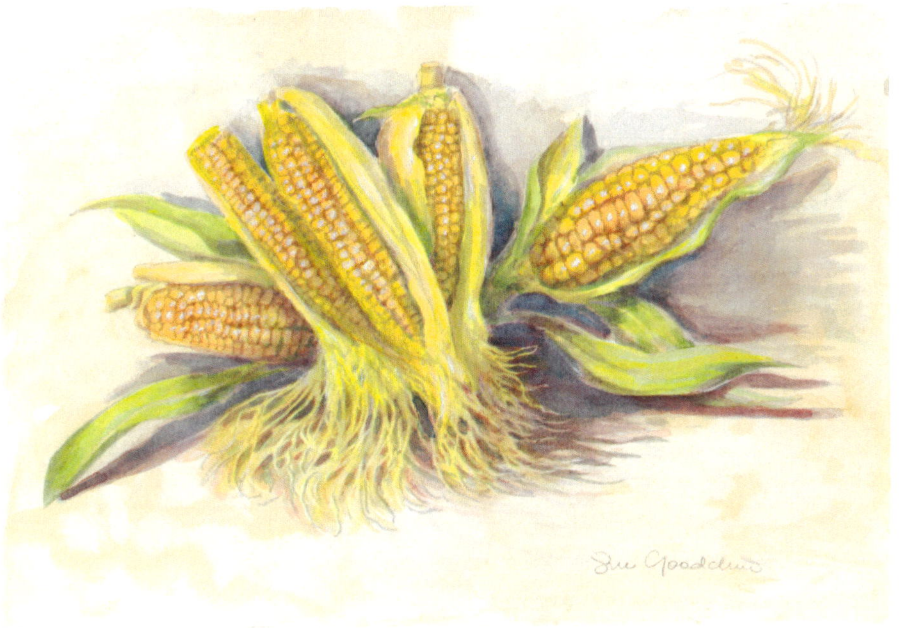

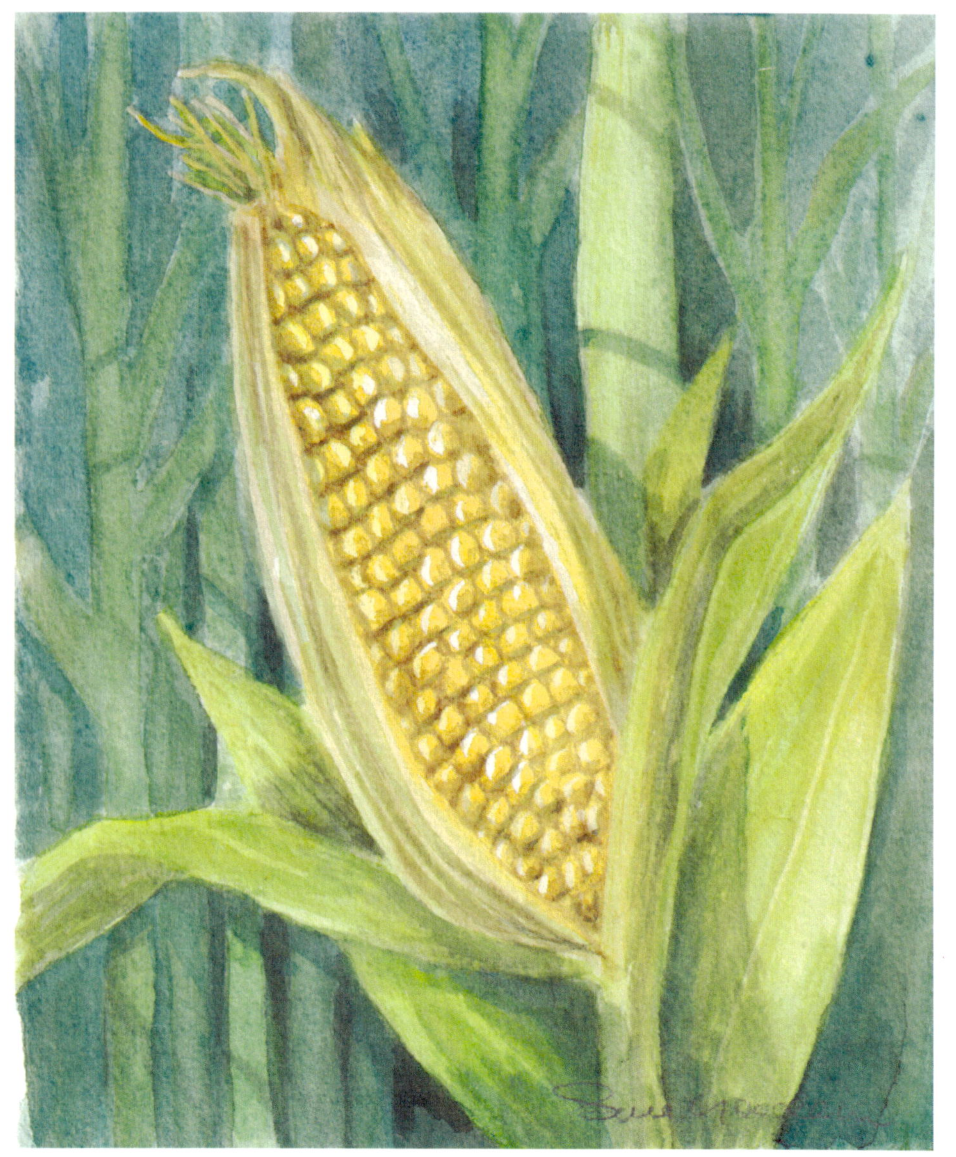

The background was initially a wash of Ultramarine Blue overpainted with different strengths of green but this green, appears bluer than the foreground because the cool underpainting is overpainted with more cool colours.

On assessing the values, I darkened various tones by adding a wash of Phthalo Blue and lightened others with Lemon Yellow. Spatial organisation of the composition helps the movement from foreground to background. The scale of foreground objects is in relation to the size of features further away. Atmospheric perspective is where colours become cooler in the distance and warm ones appear to come forward.

The Gardener
This half-hardy annual grows best in high temperatures and full sun. A soil temperature of 10°C is needed for rapid germination, but better results are obtained with transplanted plants, pre-germinated in pots during April for planting out in May.

Male and female flowers are produced in different places on the same plant. Male flowers grow at the top of the plant and female flowers, which develop into the sweetcorn cob, are lower down. They are pollinated by wind, so should be planted in a block. Pollen is produced by the male flowers in summer and falls on to the female flowers. These wither and form the cobs about a month later.

The cobs should be firm and well filled, and are ready when the silks have turned dark brown. To test for ripeness, pierce one of the grains with a thumbnail. If the liquid which emerges is pale and watery, then the cob is not ready. Close the sheath and leave to ripen a little longer. When the liquid is rich and creamy the cob is at its best and must be picked before it becomes mealy and unpalatable. Pick the cob off the plant with a sharp downward twist or cut with a knife. They are best eaten straight after harvesting.

PUMPKIN

The Painting

A relatively simple way to create a sense of drama is to exaggerate and intensify colour contrasts. Pure hues with high colour intensity give an exciting, active visual quality. The warm orange/red colours of the pumpkin have a vitality and jump out from the cool colours of its leaves, which appear more recessive. A focal point does two essential things for a painting. It attracts attention and it shows whatever is important about the subject. The colour of the pumpkin commands attention because of the colour contrast.

To help ideas and build passion, sketch the subject and try different approaches, different colours and different values and decide which works best. I didn't have to work hard with this subject as the plant was there before me, ready to paint. I exaggerated the blue in the background to help with the feeling of recession.

The Gardener

The seeds should be sown indoors and planted out in early summer in a warm, sunny place. The soil should be enriched with rich organic matter. The plants take up a lot of space, but can be grown vertically on canes with fruits supported in nets. The fruits should be cut when they are fully coloured and the skins have hardened and before the first frost. In the right conditions, they can be stored until spring.

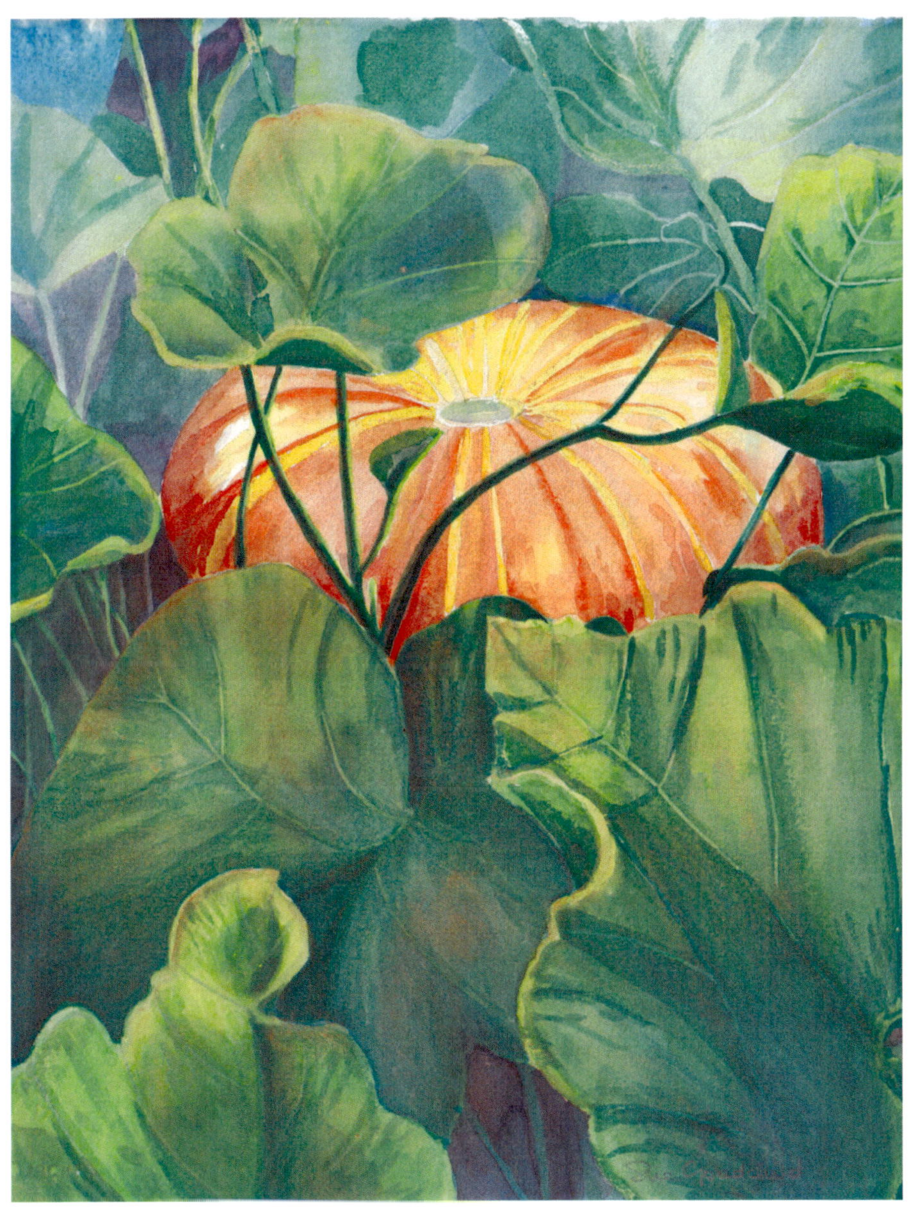

Pumpkins are very nutritional, being full of vitamins A, C and E, fibre, carotene and zinc. They are good against heart disease, hypertension and cancer. The seeds contain protein and essential fatty acids. Pumpkins can be cooked in many ways – roasted, boiled, and in stews and curries.

LEEKS

The Drawing

With the paper attached to a board, I chose which coloured pencils to use. The initial drawing of the outline was made with Sap Green followed by shading in the darks and shadows with Mineral Green. This needs careful planning as the drawing cannot easily be changed. I began with a tonal drawing with the darkest values, then

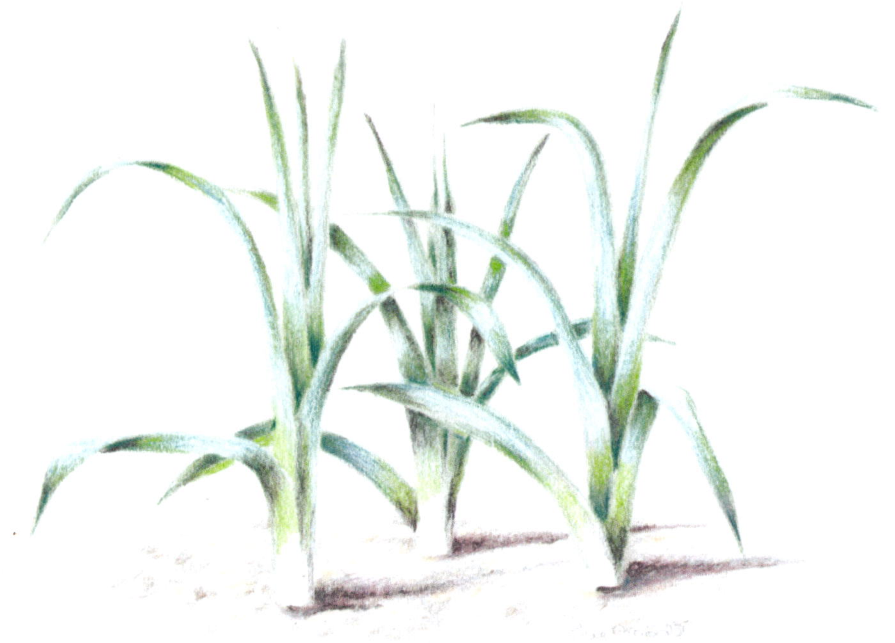

the mid tones and chose to leave the lights as unpainted paper. If I were using coloured paper then light pigments would be necessary. The leaves were then blocked in with turquoise, leaving the bases as uncoloured paper. More shading was added with Mineral Green, and for the lower part of the leaves I used Grass Green. Once the lights and darks were established, more colour was added using greater pressure with successive layers. The ground was simply scribbles with Raw Sienna and then Sepia, leaving some Sienna uncovered. The shadows across the ground from the leeks were Red Violet Lake using the most pressure at the base of the plants. Touches of Bottle Green were dotted into the shadows as a colour link from ground to plants.

Coloured pencils are an exciting medium, but demand forethought, discipline and patience to build up the layers. It is a challenge to make the darks dark enough without using black, but black can be used before adding colour. Some artists blend the pigments with a bristle brush, which pushes the pigment into the tooth of the paper, making it appear more like paint.

The Gardener
Leeks are easily raised from seed sown in mid spring in shallow drills with plants usually planted in late summer or early autumn following other crops. As leeks are deep-rooted, they do not suffer too much from drought so long as there is sufficient compost, but they do benefit from a good soaking. The edible part of the leek is the blanched stem, which contains high beneficial phytonutrients in the green part. This can be increased by drawing dry, friable soil up the stems, being careful that it docs not fall into the heart of the plant. They can be harvested in

winter. Leeks continue to grow slowly in cold weather; but if left until spring, a surge of new growth culminates in seed heads.

PARSNIPS

The Painting

Deciding how to portray the parsnips posed questions. Should I paint them growing in the garden, which would mean only showing leaves with the roots underground? Should the roots be grouped together or should there be just one? Or should they have their foliage still attached? I decided to include some foliage to add colour and texture to the painting of the pale roots.

I used very few colours: a wash of Yellow Ochre, the shadows darkened with Burnt Umber and warmed with Burnt Sienna. When dry darkened further with Permanent violet. These colours were used in the surround and then a washy Lemon Yellow was used to highlight the roots on one side and the light source coming from the right.

The Gardener

Parsnips are among the first crops to be sown and the last to be harvested. They need deep soil – preferably not stony, which causes forking – which should not have been manured for at least a year before sowing. They have a low nitrogen requirement and need soil as loose as possible so that air can penetrate to the greatest depth. The best position is sunny, but some shade is tolerated. Except in a drought, they do not need watering.

Sow fresh seed in spring, avoiding cold, wet weather. If the weather is dry, water the drill before sowing. Germination can be a problem; but by covering the seed

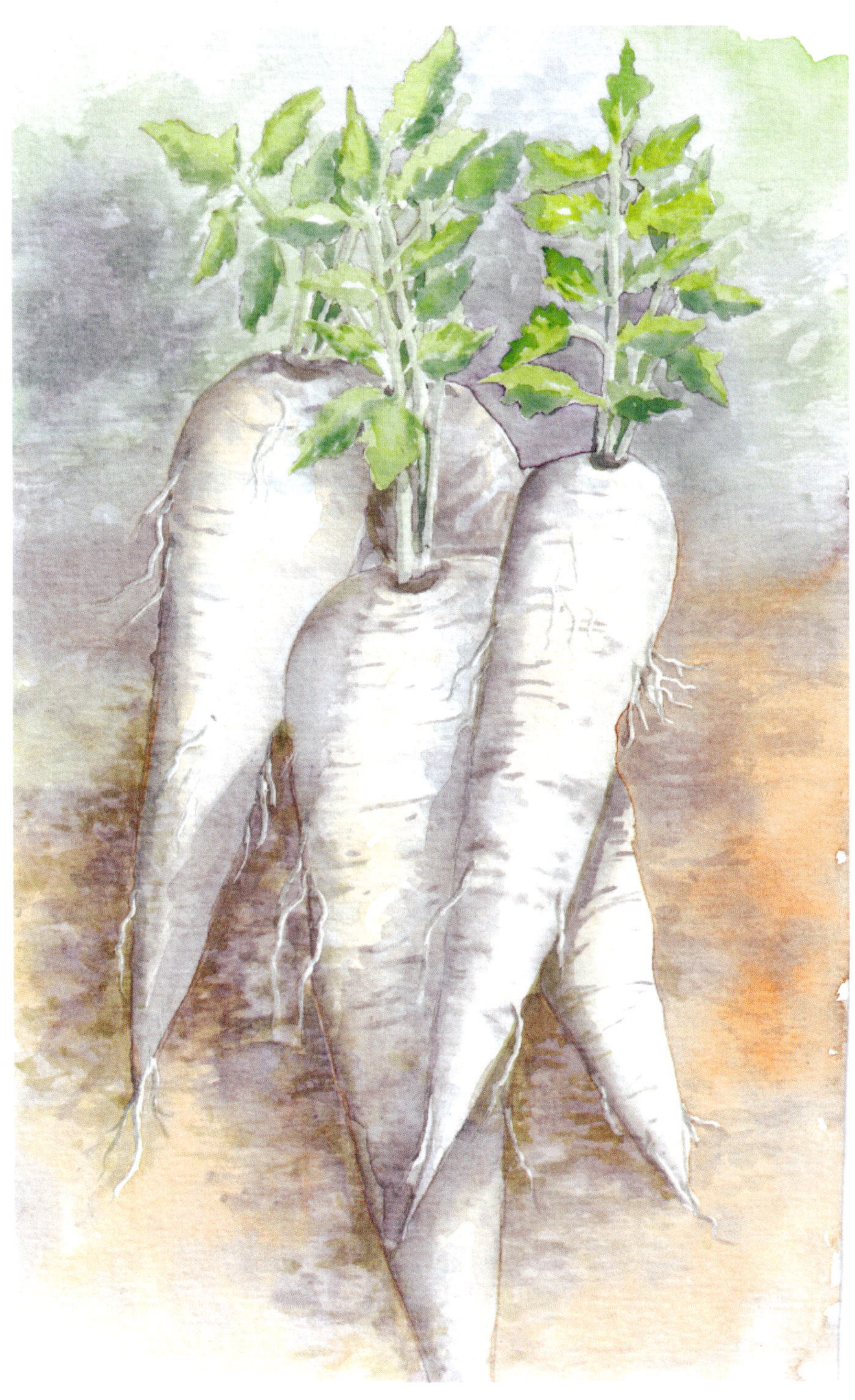

with cardboard for a few weeks, moisture will be retained. It is a good idea to sow the seed along with radish seeds, which germinate quickly and show the parsnip row. Radishes can be harvested a few weeks later. Parsnips need plenty of space to swell into good-sized roots.

Lifting may begin once the foliage begins to die down. Parsnips can be left in the ground over winter when it is said that a frost improves the flavour.

THE ARTIST AND THE GARDENER

I'm not a botanical illustrator, where everything has to be exactly correct, but I revel in painting what is before me whether it has a crinkled leaf or a caterpillar hole. There is something very exciting about the colours of marigolds and nasturtiums or poppies growing among the vegetables, and I delight in harvesting among the flowers, even if it means spoiling the glorious colours of nature's arrangement.

In the garden my sense of design comes through in composing, placing one shape next to another, enhancing one colour or complementing another, and this comes from my love of painting. Gardening is painting with plants, whether it be different colours and shapes or using a certain position to make an ordinary plant appear dramatic or exciting. The garden is the canvas, the sketchbook or the watercolour paper, but it is also a setting for my husband's fish ponds – and, thankfully, he is very good at cutting the grass. These swathes of restful green set off the rest of the garden and give us pleasure to share with friends, birds, insects and, of course, our beautiful St Bernard.

It is the most irresistible thrill to walk around the garden, to see how the flower borders change, sometimes overnight, and how the vegetables plump up and recover from wind and frost and revel in the spring sunshine.

When I take time out in the garden, I may not be painting, but gathering inspiration and ideas. And although I enjoy sowing, planting and weeding, I look forward to hours in the studio. I try to paint the life force of living plants, interpreting reality. Painting and gardening are an all-consuming passion, challenging but enormous fun. And although both require patience, they are exciting. Composing living pictures is a highly creative, multidimensional art form. It is hard work, happy work with endless creativity, ever changing, ever delighting.